FOR HOLISTIC WELLNESS IN HEALTH, WEALTH, RELATIONS, CAREER, MONEY & PERSONALITY

(WITH SPECIAL SECTION ON MEMORY TECHNIQUES)

# THE BLISS

I0414870

(VOLUME -1)

## TOUCHING & EMPOWERING HEARTS!

## WITH

## NEURO LINGUISTIC PROGRAMMING &

## EMOTIONAL INTELLIGENCE

### BY VAIBHAV VASANT PATIL &

### SHRUTI DHRUVE CHITLANGIA

SHARE SKILLS
Center For Training & Transformation

- **BOOK NAME:** The Bliss -Touching & Empowering Hearts
- **©SHARESKILLS CENTER FOR TRAINING & TRANSFORMATION**

- **ISBN :**9788194156710

- **AUTHORS:**

  Vaibhav Vasant Patil & Shruti Chitlangia Dhruve

- **PUBLISHER:**
  **Shareskillsonline**

- **Proof reading:**

  Dr.Yogesh Anvekar

- **PRINTED BY:**

  Rahul Printers, Karad, District Satara, 415110

- **FIRST EDITION:**

  5th July 2019

- **SECOND VERSION :**

- **Audiobook & E book :**

- 5th July 2020

- **PRICE:**
  E-Book: 200/-, Audiobook: 300/- , Paperback: 400,
  kindle E- Book: 205/-

# ACKNOWLEDGEMENT (From Author)

I would like to dedicate this book to my parents – my mother Asha Vasant Patil & my father Vasant Pandurang Patil,because till now even after my struggle for success they have always supported me, kept faith in me & my abilities. They always gave priority to education for me and my sister and today only because of their lifelong sacrifice and efforts we both are highly educated. I am also especially thankful to my father who gave me many opportunities to conduct trainings in government organizations through his goodwill and contacts. I am also thankful to my sister Priyanka Patil-Alekar for her motherly love and care and her words of wisdom.

Last but most important , I am thankful to Shruti Chitlangia Dhruve - my copartner in my training company- Shareskills and also who authored with me in our book-'The Bliss'. Shruti and my skills are complementary to each other which bring in perfection, quality with quantity to all our training programs. She has a lion's share in writing this book and raising its standards through her values, virtues and vision this book is a result of consistent hard work and experience through our diverse training programs and brain teasing sessions.

I along with Shruti Chitlangia Dhruve sincerely thank Prof. Yogesh Anvekar for his valuable inputs while drafting this book & also for proof reading the content of the book & make it error free.

Also we thank Mr. Rajan Pendulkar of Gaurang Publishing for helping us in publishing this book.

We thank our team who took care of our company while we were engaged in writing this book.

We are thankful for our gurus & mentors-Tony Robbins, late Dr. Joseph Murphy & the trainers from whom we took training & guidance for mindfulness.

We are also thankful to the authors whose books we read & could prepare our own content for this book.

We thank from the bottom of our heart to all our students and our participants from public & corporate workshops from whom we have been learning immensely with their experiences & feedbacks. Their appreciations & acknowledgement for their core transformation have been real motivation & energy boosters for us.

**"Keep Hopes alive"-Vaibhav Vasant Patil**

# ACKNOWLEDGEMENT (From Author)

I want to dedicate this book to my father Krishnamurari Chitlangia who has been my real hero & idol. Whatever I am today is only because of the virtues, values, discipline, good habits he inculcated & nurtured into me.

We can't excel in our professional life if things are not well settled in our personal life. Work-life balance is quite essential to prosper in life. I am thankful to my beloved husband Nirav Dhruve for standing firm beside me in ups & downs of life. Life seemed a roller coaster ride but due to his company & support, life was all the more smooth. He made sure that I get enough time to vegetate on my thoughts and write this book

I would say 'a mother is also born newly along with her child'. Yes, I am thankful to almighty & this universe to gift me with motherhood & my son Khavish. Khavish means lord Ganesh & as we start our any new work with blessings of lord Ganesha, I started my new career which was more challenging & versatile with 100 times more energy & dedication with my little Ganesha ! He has been true motivation behind my immense energy.

I extend my infinite thanks to my mother Saroj Krishnamurari Chitlangia for the shower of love and care on me. I had contemplated to write this book long back and I had gone through a lot of books, websites, blogs and YouTube videos and utilized my time in productive way, which was possible due to her consistent availability for me & my baby. I always felt empowered & stronger with her.

I am equally indebted to my beloved parents in law. I extend my sincere thanks to my mother in law Rekha Kirit Dhruve and my father in law Kirit Dhruve as they always supported me in all possible ways and treated me like their own daughter. They always took care to keep environment in home resourceful, playful, happy and harmonious due to which all of us could excel in our professional life with excellent work -life balance.

I am thankful to my co-author of this book & founder of Shareskills Mr.Vaibhav Vasant Patil sir for his dedication & passion with which he accompanied me in the journey of publishing this book. His energy, intellectual capabilities, creativity, commitment are just exceptional. Along with me he has been excellent mastermind of this book for its operational proceedings right from drafting it on paper with pen till its printing & publishing.

**"Keep Hopes alive"-Shruti Chitlangia Dhruve**

# TABLE OF CONTENTS

**SECTIONS**                                    **PAGE**
**NUMBERS**

Acknowledgement...................................................................4

Preface ..............................................................................10


**PART 1: The Bliss with Neuro Linguistic Programming**

Chapter 1.1: Introduction to NLP......................................14

Chapter 1.2: Removing past painful memories.................33

Chapter 1.3: Empowering limiting
beliefs.........................41

Chapter 1.4: Transforming self........................................54

Chapter 1.5: Anchoring & conditioning mind...................67


**Part 2: The Bliss with Emotional Intelligence**

Chapter 2.1: Introduction to EI........................................84

Chapter 2.2: Thinking empathetically.............................101

Chapter 2.3: Building rapport with people.....................113

Chapter 2.4: Changing state of mind................................124

Chapter 2.5: Living in present........................................135


**Part 3: The Bliss with Memory Techniques**

Chapter 3.1: Memory techniques as NLP application...148


**PART 4: About the creators of 'The Bliss'**

About Shareskills & Shareskillsonline............................178

Testimonials by clients.....................................................192

About  Vaibhav Vasant Patil.............................................201

About Shruti Chitlangia Dhruve .......................................206

Get in touch with us..........................................................211

## *KEEP HOPES ALIVE!*

# PREFACE (By Authors)

It is my pleasure to extend our knowledge and expertise gathered over the last 10 years by means of our **comprehensive life & career skills book**. We have revised, filtered and bettered the contents multiple times hence we are sure this book will not only touch but empower your hearts.

**The Bliss represents overall wellness in life!** After spending soo many years in training industry and after transforming over lakhs of people, we have realized that topics such as subconscious mind, NLP, Emotional Intelligence, Memory Techniques are perceived to be meant for specific class of people only. But with our public workshops, online trainings and especially with our book, we are determined to devote our lives for spreading awareness and training people at mass level on the 'power of subconscious mind' for betterment in personal & professional life of people because it is inherent, irrespective of their financial condition, profession, qualifications or caste.

The USP or the differentiation factor of this book from other NLP or Emotional Intelligence books is that-we have given **abundant techniques along with our personal experiences**, so that the readers of this book can practice NLP & Emotional Intelligence techniques by themselves. A special section on memory techniques as an application of NLP has also been incorporated towards the end.

These memory techniques are applicable for school and college studies or even in corporate life. We sincerely believe that our dear readers who have invested their money & time should get exceed their expectations- a content which is a mix of knowledge, activities, stories & our personal experiences. We have taken a special care that the language of this book is understandable to any individual irrespective of his or her age. Besides we have tried our level best to make this an interactive book for our readers.

The bliss -Touching & Empowering Hearts is available in various versions such as **kindle, E book, and book and paper back.** The bliss is also available in **Hindi and Marathi** version. The first version of bliss consists of NLP, Emotional Intelligence and Memory Techniques applied to important domains of life such as health, career, relationships, profession, money and mindfulness. The upcoming **series of 'The Bliss'** will focus more upon **in depth and advanced level** of NLP, Emotional Intelligence and Memory Techniques where each of these topics will be covered with its standalone book. We would also like to declare that **the pocket versions of this book in English, Hindi & Marathi** are also going to get published soon. The advanced level volume version of 'The Bliss' is already in drafting phase, which is going to be a **'Multicolor Edition'** with more innovative techniques.

The Bliss is published by training company **Shareskills Center for Training & Transformation** and written by its founders **Mr.Vaibhav Vasant Patil & Shruti Chitlangiya Dhruve.** It is a renowned brand for corporate trainings, public workshops and institutes and college level trainings. Under this brand, trainings modules are created and delivered in various fields by our expert team of trainers. The mission of our organizations Shareskills Trainings is to work for masses and our vision is that every human being must be aware of and utilize the skills & power which lies within self. Everyone has the right to live a blissful life and no one should suffer from health, mind, career, relationships or monetary issues.

We will feel blessed if this book can bring a transformation in your life - which we are confident about. Although we have given our best and taken care of technical soundness of the book, still errors, feedbacks, suggestions, appreciations, critiques from you for the betterment of this book are welcome. If you wish to clarify any query regarding concepts or techniques in this book, then you may send an email which will be answered within 48 hours.

We wish you happiness, prosperity, success, love, health and wealth for your life! Before you start reading this book, Find a mirror, look into it, keep your thumbs up & say loudly, **"Keep Hopes Alive"**!

# *PART 1*

# *THE BLISS*

# *WITH*

# *NEURO LINGUISTIC PROGRAMMING*

# CHAPTER 1.1

# INTRODUCTION TO NLP

How will you feel if we offer you a magical genie like Aladdin had in his lamp, who will give you whatever you want in your life at your wish? Isn't it amazing? And let us tell you friends that it is for real and not fantasy!

Yes, what we just told you is 100% true! First of all, let us both congratulate you for taking the initiative to transform your life & bring pleasant 'Bliss' in your life!

What is bliss? Bliss is a perfect happiness, delight, boundless joy, being on seventh heaven, a feeling of being on cloud nine; a feeling of euphoria & ecstasy-all happy go lucky terms for life!

May we ask you how will you get this holistic happiness/bliss in your life? Friends, what is your problem? What are problems which most people are facing? Yes, what you are thinking is absolutely in the right direction! People are happy or sad in their life only because of deficiency of certain common things in life which are health, wealth, relations, career, money & the lack of some personality traits! Isn't it? So, we mean to say that you can make your life 'blissful' if you can bring wellness in those important aspects of life! We are going to give you a gift trio in terms of lifelong tools which are going to give you healthy body, issueless mind, cordial relations, work/ life balance, bright career, abundant money & a better version of your personality. Yes, and these gifts are –NLP (Neuro Linguistic Programming), EI (Emotional Intelligence) & MT (Memory Techniques). Let us begin with NLP first which is related with our subconscious mind!

**THE SECRET POWER OF SUBCONSCIOUS MIND:**

This secret of success or failure of a human being is the miraculous - working power found in his or her own subconscious mind. You can bring into your life more power, more wealth, more health, more happiness, and more joy by learning to contact and unleash the hidden latent power of your subconscious mind. You just need to bring awareness of & implement this power of subconscious mind. Through the wisdom of subconscious mind, you can attract good health, abundant wealth, harmonious relations, excellent memory power, bright career & anything you desire. You just need to believe in you & communicate your desires to your subconscious mind consistently & with conviction, **so that it will go deep in your subconscious mind & then via conscious**

**mind your brain & this universe will bless you with fulfillment of your desires & wishes.**

## WHAT IS SUBCONSCIOUS MIND?

Let's understand the subconscious mind with an example of driving. While learning to drive, we use our conscious mind. We consciously pay attention to accelerator, brakes & clutch whereas it gets difficult to focus on road & traffic, but, once over a period of time, the driving skills goes deep into our subconscious mind due to consistency & repetitive efforts to consciously learn it,  and finally we can drive in a smooth way with utmost comfort level. In fact we can do multiple tasks such as talking with people sitting in our car. Same goes for any learning process like studies, swimming, cooking, music etc.

Our body's internal mechanisms are controlled by our subconscious mind such as breathing, heartbeats, digestive system, lungs, kidneys etc. A simple example can be whenever we get any injury or wound on our limbs, there exists the power of subconscious mind to heal it without any medicine as healing is basic to our nature .This is used by the subconscious mind and you can see the wound disappears within a  few weeks. This is also applicable for curing some diseases like cough, colds etc., where without any medicine, with the help of the immune power & mechanism of our body the subconscious mind cures those illnesses.

The subconscious mind **never sleeps** because even in our sleep our body mechanisms run- we dream, we sweat while sleeping, our hair, nails, muscles continue to grow during sleep which is controlled by incessant subconscious mind which is much more powerful than conscious mind. There are evidences showing that our subconscious mind while we are in deep sleep at night, takes major decisions which indicates that subconscious mind is active even if we are sleeping hence we should not miss any such event or decision which subconscious mind makes us see or feel while are sleeping.

## WHAT IS CONSCIOUS MIND?

The conscious mind is more about what currently we are focusing & thinking rationally and logically. A common example is when you attend any lecture, you tend to see, write & hear the teacher's delivery with your conscious mind where you control your attention. Your conscious mind is the master controller of your body, internal environment, and all your thought process. Your subconscious mind receives commands that your conscious mind gives to it depending upon your beliefs. The conscious mind sleeps when human being sleeps unlike the subconscious mind. The conscious mind essentially puts any thoughts or actions at subconscious level. When you consciously consistently say to people, "I can't do it", then your subconscious mind takes your words & sees to it that you will not be in a position to do what you want & desire". **Events which happen in our life are 'received' with conscious mind & 'perceived' & 'stored' at subconscious mind level.**

## WHAT IS UNCONSCIOUS MIND?

Our unconscious mind comprises of mental processes that are not accessible & controllable by the consciousness mind but that influence our decision making, judgments, feelings, or behavior. The unconscious mind is the primary driver of human behavior. Like an iceberg, the most important part of the mind is the part you cannot see at deeper level. Our beliefs, feelings, motives, patterns and decisions are actually influenced by our past experiences and stored in the unconscious as well as subconscious mind. It is very difficult to access & control our unconscious mind where deep counseling & programming, professional help is required. We are fully aware of what is going on in our conscious mind; but we have no idea of what information is stored in the unconscious mind.

(Image source: By Moteoo from Pixabay)

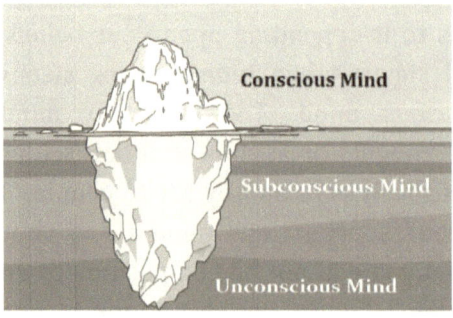

**The iceberg analogy of conscious, subconscious & unconscious mind.**

## DDG THEORY

**DDG Stands for Deletion, Distortion & Generalization.** Our mind does DDG while perceiving events. We have 2 things with us from birth i.e. body and mind which run multiple processes of body and results in growth. All our organs are run by this software of mind. This software has been given extra space which is called memory which is made up of 80 billion neurons are spread across all body in the form of electrifying neural networks of nervous system. Problems happen when in this space we start feeding viruses over the period of time instead of relevant things. Now virus is damaging software which was not meant for growth and positive things.

In life, events are going on since our birth such as people loving or hating us, occurrences happening around us. Our mind is receiving events with our FIVE SENSES i.e. Eyes (Visual), Ears (Auditory), Nose (Olfactory), Tongue (Gustatory) & kinesthetic sense for feelings and touch (Muscles and skin). All these five senses are meant to ensure smoothness and safety in our day to day activities. All feelings are lying in your kinesthesia; we can feel feelings in our muscles. The feeling is in our body that's why our body gets affected due to feeling. For example, we get perspiration due to a feeling of fear. What a wonderful system we have! Each event of life should have been preserved in the mind but our mind deletes some things. Every day you see lot of cars and people but our mind forgets it. We receive lakhs of things with five senses everyday but retain very few. Any information we first take with five senses - our mind then deletes that information before it gets stored in our mind. For example when you say," I am depressed", that time you delete the possibility of an opportunity to solve the problem. Our mind distorts some things at the time of reception & perceives events with a changed meaning.

Generalization means you have some past learning, information, opinions from other people or media such as TV, newspaper, beliefs and you are doing all things with respect to that belief only. For example, in your childhood, you listen that the son of your neighbor is ruined due to money, and then it affirmed your belief that, 'money is a bad thing'.

**There are two types of beliefs:**

**1) Universal Truth      2) Random Generalized Truth**

Example: The earth revolves around the sun is universal truth; nobody will dispute this universal truth

Example: Our daily thoughts and beliefs are random generalized truths such as 'Money spoils life'.

We should not follow random generalized truth and get rid of it. In NLP we program our neurons to get rid of negative generalized truth. Event A is a general event which happened with all people, but everyone perceives that event differently & put in their mind. We delete, distort and generalize event A and it gets converted into event B which is called as perception i.e. our personal reception. Event A is common to all & is objective experience & Event B is subjective experience. Husband and wife fights on the basis of subjective experience. Perception always wins over reality. Our mind programs information. B is also called as internal map or subconscious-imprint or pattern or neural pathway. If Event B is filled with your past guilt, revenge, break ups then it results in illness.

Event B is giving you state of mind which is also called as energy, zone, mood or form. State can be positive or resourceful or negative or unresourceful. Happiness, good decision making, loving someone are positive states and sadness, insecurity, confusion, phobia are all negative states. When we are in positive state then we use all our resources from mind and body for our health, wealth, relations, career& money and ensure everything is going smoothly that's why it is called as resourceful state. When you are in negative state even if you have resources you don't get state to use those skills and state is formed by our neurons and mind programming. Negative state is like you have crores of rupees in your cupboard but as you don't have the key, you can't remove even 1rupee. **People don't lack resources but they lack 'resourceful state'.** Parents, children, couples need resourceful state. A person who says I am depressed lacks it .If we lack this state, we should always act and take action and communicate. Our action or communication can be:

**1. Verbal action**-It has action verbs like I will sleep, I will die. I will get affected etc. Verbal action or communication is majorly based upon words, sentences, commands etc. In NLP & EI while doing activities. We use verbal actions & communications at initial stage.

**2. Nonverbal action**- It consists of actions related with our body such as Physiology or body language, heat beats, reddening of face when you get angry. Whatever action you will take, will create results. Results will give you destiny or disaster; hence Non verbal action is equally important. Example if you get ill, then it results in lack of money. Without memory our life doesn't have memory. In NLP we change event B and bring wellness in our life.

**WHAT IS NLP?**

**NLP –Neuro Linguistic Programming** is a programming language for subconscious mind where we primarily use our five senses, to control & transform our thoughts & belief systems. Neuro means related to brain & Neurons. Neurons are cells within the nervous system that transmit information to other nerve cells, muscle, or glands. In NLP we program our mind so that neurons & brain functions for our desired outputs. Linguistic means related to language. We use specific language in NLP, to give relevant signals to Neurons as per our wish & wants. Programming is the specific language where we use our five senses & conscious mind to change, transform, manage or improve certain things in subconscious mind. With NLP, we can bring holistic wellness in our Health, Wealth, Relations, and Career & Business.

## SUBMODALITIES

Let's take an example: Go into an event which was delightful such as your marriage or any picnic or outing, party etc. Go into the event. Now start thinking answers of following question.

1. Is the image still or moving?

2. Is it colorful or black and white?

3. Is it panoramic or frame?

4. Is image is 3D or 2D?

4. Is it close or far?

5. Where is location of images? Left, right or front?

This event A has gone. **And the qualities which we explore about event B** are nothing but sub-modalities. The ways you have perceived with neurons are your visual qualities.NLP takes structure and not actual content. Sub modalities also indicate your interests in any particular thing, it will tell grass root level cause of illness or any mental trauma. In NLP we refer qualities as modalities. And with respect to five senses they are called sub-modalities. **Every person has perception i.e. personal reception of Event B;** event A is same for all. NLP with the help of sub modalities, programs our mind. As far as the things with which you are emotionally attached, your sub modalities are bright and bold such as big size, colorful, loud voice etc. & when you are not emotionally associated with anything, then sub modalities associated with those things are weak and blurred such as black and white, low voice, closed view etc. Sub-modalities are nothing but the **quality of our VAK (Visual, Auditory & Kinesthetic senses).**

Your mind has a combination of this VAK for this particular thing. Your memory is made up of these three things for that thing which results in affection, love for that thing. These qualities of visual, audio and kinesthetic senses are called sub-modalities. Every person has different sub modalities for same objects or things depending on perception of each person.

**WHY IS NLP REQUIRED?**

Every human being on this earth should know how to use NLP to give positive signals & vibes to neurons & subconscious mind, to come out of past memories, to create resources to solve problems, to build confidence, to memorize things in a specific way, for self transformation, to reduce anxiety, to empower mind association/dissociation/reframing, to break allergy patterns, to raise career graph & efficiency, to make money, to change beliefs, to get rid of addictions & bad habits, to model ourselves on the basis of the excellence of other successful people. On a concluding note, we can say that to bring overall wellness in six important domains of life which are health, wealth, relations, career & memory, NLP is most essential tool.

## HOW CAN WE IMPLEMENT NLP IN DAILY LIFE?

By learning the programming language for our neurons & subconscious mind, with techniques based on using our five senses such as anchoring, rapport building, deletion, distortion & generalizations, we can make our own techniques also on the basis of our requirements & available resources.

## WHAT IS THE LAW OF ATTRACTION?

This universe & we all are governed by certain universal laws such as law of gravity which are always true & if we consciously see our life, we can sense the presence of universal laws. The law of attraction is also one of them which simply mean we always attract things in our life on whatever we focus our conscious attention & put that thing in our subconscious mind level. In Hindi there is a famous saying **"Kehte hain agar kisi cheez ko sacche dil se chaho ... to poori kainath use tumse milane ki koshish mein lag jaati hai"** (It means if you truly desire something from your heart. Then the entire universe helps you in trying to connect with it)

With Subconscious mind & NLP, we can attract wellness in any area we want. **The Law of Attraction uses the power of the mind to transform whatever is in our thoughts and materialize them into reality.** You might have also experienced this law in your life. At least once in life you must have attracted a person or thing towards yourself, about which you were constantly thinking with passion & focused attention such as wife, prize, job, friends, surprises , car, home, health etc.

## A) COMMAND ON HEALTH:

It is said that **'A Healthy Mind in a Healthy Body'**, **'Health Is Wealth'**. Everything good in our life is connected with good health. Every achievement, every good relation is a waste if your health is not good to experience & feel the whole hearted joy of it.

### 'RAINBOW FISHES' TECHNIQUE FOR HEALTH:

This technique is to be used for overall internal healing for infections, virus, hormonal imbalance etc. & external body related healing aspects. This is a simple NLP technique where we are using our senses. Do this activity when you are travelling, waiting in queue or before you sleep. You need to get more associative with your subconscious mind & more dissociative with your conscious mind before doing this activity.

- Close your eyes & feel relaxation from top to bottom in your body.
- Once you feel completely relaxed, take your right hand towards your left side of chest & while doing this imagine you are giving yourself all important resources in the form of colors which can heal you internally & externally also  such as immunity, needed multivitamins, proteins, blessings of your god etc.

- Now imagine, thousands of small colorful fishes with all those healing resources are originated in your heart & brain.
- Now some are travelling from within your blood veins, some from muscles & some from bones towards your brain. Imagine those fishes are rejuvenating your hormone secretion with all healthy, good, happiness & love hormones such as endorphins, Serotonin, Dopamine, Oxytocin & they are freezing the process of bad, unhealthy hormones such as adrenaline & cortical etc. Those fishes are giving massage to your hair roots with their tongue & nourishing them with needed elements for growth. Then those fishes are travelling to your eyes, their temperature is cold & they are giving pleasurable cold feel to your eyes. They are cleaning your eyes & supplying needed vitamins such as vitamin A to area around the eyes. They are making your eyes shine. Then they are travelling to your hand. They are healing your wound if any & they are strengthening your muscles, giving powerful internal massage to your hands muscles tissues, bones, veins etc. & you may continue enjoying the journey of rainbow fishes throughout your body in a similar manner.
- Feel the healing touch, magical movements of fishes in your body. Intensify it with more concentration.
- Create belief that you are getting the much needed healing & your health issues are being solved by

rainbow fishes. Reflect this belief of being healed in your body with smiling face, confident shoulders, erect spine etc.

- Repeat this process daily. It will prepare your body & subconscious mind for more effective & faster healing & boost any medical therapy at its best.

(**Note:** Join our advance NLP course for learning & practically experiencing commands with more detailed approach.)

## ONE NLP TIP FOR WELLNESS

• Chunk down your language with self. For example, if you say, 'I am having diabetes it means,' I am Diabetic' ,but if you are having a pen then does it means that,' I am having pen = I am Pen?'. For diabetes you can chunk down your language as, 'I am having a temporary body condition with little more sugar level which is called as diabetes'. Let's consider one more example, For earning 1 crore rupees in a year you can chunk down your language & say,' I want to earn 100 lakh rupees' as your mind is more acquainted with lakhs rather than crores if you are from middle class or upper middle class family. Another example can be- instead of saying, sorry for making you wait, you can say thank you for waiting.

## PERSONAL EXPERIENCE ON NLP

As you all know, the toughest phase for a woman comes when she is about to become a mother. Pregnancy phase is bliss, but with it comes lot of relevant negative aspects such as physical change, weight gain, hair loss, mood swings, frequent vomiting, family pressure(due to extra care), medicine schedules, worries about healthy delivery and post-delivery phase.

I was extremely happy when I confirmed about my pregnancy news, but the next moment all those negative things just struck my mind. I had always taken care about my diet, my appearance and had kept weight in check, but once I realized that my weight will clock almost 90 KGs due to my height, I was scared to imagine my looks. But the very next thought came to my mind, 'Shruti, why are you worried? You are a NLP Trainer and Emotional Intelligence Expert, what is the use of your knowledge and skills about NLP and Emotional Intelligence, when you cannot apply them in your own life?' At that very moment I decided to spend my pregnancy phase in reading more NLP and Emotional Intelligence contents from books, internet and started applying it on myself. I could remember, I along with my colleague designed almost 40 NLP & Emotional Intelligence techniques and made sure they are super effective in term of results.

See friends, the first mistake we do is that we expect quick results in our life. This never happens in reality but gradually if you start visualizing, things start happening and this is what I did during the important phase of my life. My cousins, friends told me that pregnancy and post-delivery is time where almost every women go through depression, trauma and lots of physical and mental problems, but as I said earlier during my pregnancy, I was 100% sure that I will never let any such negativities affect my life. That is where after 2 months I started stepping out of my house for a walk. Gradually I increased it to 15 minutes, half an hour and then to 1 hour. As it was my feeding phase, I had to return back home. With all my visualization, expertise and understanding, I started handling both the things simultaneously. These small but effective steps, my affirmations and my strength did not let me give up and in this journey my family helped me a lot. I was alone at the beginning but later I was supported with my family people and that was possible only because I did not give up and applied all the knowledge first on myself. I can say with my entire conviction that I can apply it on any women who need strength, because 'strength is not what you see outside; it lies within you. You just have to believe in it'. I started visualizing my phases during and after pregnancy. I started my every day with affirmations such as, "I will be having normal delivery and healthy child". I started visualizing face, eyes of my baby. It gave me feeling of happiness, gratitude, satisfaction, thankfulness to this universe for blessing me with healthy baby during my pregnancy. Many times it happened that I went to the hospital for my routine check-ups alone without my family or relatives accompanying me, but then at that time, I used all my emotional intelligence techniques and empathetic thinking techniques due to which I could manage to maintain my pleasant mindset which was important for my baby's healthy growth. As you must be knowing that many women leave their careers voluntarily, forcefully or helplessly during initial and post pregnancy phase. I wanted to resume with my career post pregnancy. It was going to be challenging, but I prepared my mind by giving positive signals to my neural pathway with affirmations and visualizations, as said rightly; 'if you demand something from the universe with faith and conviction, it gets fulfilled.'

This could not have worked otherwise, but the entire journey of pregnancy phase was bliss for me from a normal woman to a stronger superwoman as that experience made me stronger and made me believe more in NLP and EI techniques. I can assure all the women that it is the strongest tool for everyone and any woman to apply it in their life. If me, being in that phase, can overcome it so blissfully and well, I can assure that any woman can and will be able to see the world with optimistic eyes and stronger belief post pregnancy and delivery phase.

**-Shruti Chitlangia Dhruve**

My son came in this world at the same time when my NLP& EI research & initial phase of book was going on.He has been my motivation & source of energy-Shruti Dhruve Chitlangia

*"Today you may select not to be the person who you were yesterday! Our life is the result of what we think in our subconscious mind today"-Vaibhav Vasant Patil*

## CHAPTER 1.2

## *REMOVING PAST PAINFUL MEMORIES*

Do you wake up in morning with painful dreams & memories? Does your past is holding you back from excelling ahead in your life? Do you cry when you are on bed, alone at home or during travelling? Do you always feel that if your past would have been different, then your present & future would have been much better?

Friends, all of us have some painful memories which limit our self -beliefs and affect our efficiency in the present. Today let us break the shackles of past & heal our mind to take giant leap for progress in our life.

**WHAT ARE PAST PAINFUL MEMORIES?**

Past painful memories are bad memories such as flashbacks, nightmares and severe anxiety, as well as uncontrollable thoughts about the past bad memories. These bad memories cause significant problems in social life, work situations and in relationships. They also become barriers for us to do even our normal daily tasks. These are events which haunts us in our present & are difficult to forget due to the intensity & impact created by them in our life. The painful event has ended many years ago, but still our mind recalls it & gets into painful, anxious & remorseful state. Events don't have actual power to give such a long lasting pain, but its perception (deletion, distortion & generalization created by our mind) gives us persistent, never ending & haunting pain. Past memory can be related with health, business, career, relationship, accident, death of a close person etc.

## WHY IS IT IMPORTANT TO REMOVE PAST PAINFUL MEMORIES?

Although it is not easy, but it is essential to remove our past painful memories & ensure we take a lesson from that painful event & using those lessons in present & future. Deleting negative memories is the best precautionary tool for treating Post Traumatic Stress Disorders (PTSD) such as trauma, anxiety, inefficiency, relevant health issues. Coming out of our past, removes the baggage from us which is stopping us from going ahead. It improves our focus & conviction in present which brings us in resourceful state where we start using our resources in optimal way towards our overall wellness.

## HOW EXACTLY TO REMOVE PAST PAINFUL MEMORY?

It is said that time is a good healer. Apart from deleting memories, it is also important that we must learn from our past. If we have done a mistake, we should make sure we are not repeating the same mistake again.

(Image Resource: First image by Kat Jayne from Pexels & second from Pixabay)

 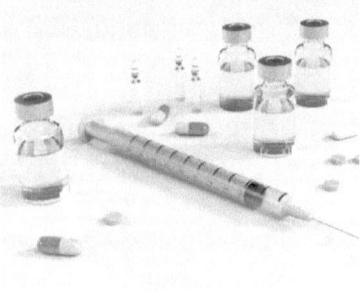

**Drugs & addiction can't be a healthy & permanent solution to remove or forget past painful memories &it is not required if you learn to reprogram your mind.**

Over a period of time, our mind learns to accept the event & then its impact on us starts diminishing-it happens generally but with some exceptions. For some people who have gone through severe past events or can't come out of their past trauma even several years after that event, this general rule does not apply. We can also think about **'what was positive intention behind the past event?'** to convert that negativity to positivity. We can commit ourselves to certain course of action or goal which will motivate us to do something positive to give a direction to our negative vibrations & negative energy towards positivity. E.g. If we have lost a close person, then we can start some social work as a token of love & attachment with that person towards a lot of positivity. We consciously delete past painful memories which requires reprogramming of our mind & manipulation of neural circuits in the brain which can be done by communicating our subconscious mind, NLP tools & techniques, or some medical treatments.

## TECHNIQUE TO IMMERSE YOUR BAD MEMORIES IN THE SEA PERMANENTLY:

- Find a place where you will not be disturbed & feel relaxed.
- Think of a bad memory which keeps disturbing you.
- You can intensify sub-modalities with your five senses (see what you saw, hear what you heard, smell what you smelled, taste what you tasted, feel what you felt) to intensify that bad memory. Make colors brighter, sounds louder, and so on.
- Focus & intensify on the visual and auditory aspects of that memory. See what you see. Hear what you can hear.
- Focus your attention on the things you can see in the memory. Which colors do you see? How close are the things to you?

- Now, you explore any positive intention behind this event. Can you find any learning behind it? Write down those learnings & positive intentions.
- Drink a glass of water and convert all those bad memories in dirty water which is accumulated in your mind and body now.
- Push this water at bottom most level in your mind. From there on this water is flowing towards your legs and then bottom most part of your leg i.e. toes.
- Then imagine that you are standing beside a big infinite and deep sea and this water of bad memories is flowing from your toes to this sea.
- This water has completely washed away from your body and getting immersed in that sea, its color is fading slowly & it has diminished deep down the sea permanently.
- Now bad memory has been completely gone away.
- What are the good & positive learnings you can gain from that bad memory?
- Keep the useful lessons and remember next time when the similar situations come.

**PERSONAL EXPERIENCE ON PAST PAINFUL MEMORY**

I have been always a topper in my school from 1st standard to 10th standard, thanks to my parents who always gave priority to my studies & made sure that I become a studious personality, for which I am grateful to them even today. It's only because of the seeds of studious nature they could sow in me during my childhood, I am reaping rich benefits of knowledge transfer in competitive exams coaching, corporate &public training industry, but unfortunately I faced one painful situation after my 10th standard board examination. I got almost 90% marks in my board exam. In those days there used to be a concept called as 'merit list' in Mumbai & Maharashtra board. I along with my some friends came in merit list with good marks, we were very happy, but I was unaware what destiny had planned for me. All of my friends got admission in the top college of Mumbai that time, but only I could not get due to caste based reservation system in India. I was in open caste & all my friends who were my colleagues since 1st standard were from reserved category. It was very painful for me to think that even if we have got same marks, I could not get admission in the top college which I have dreamed of while they could get admission only because of their caste. It was not acceptable to my mind. Still just to keep my mind & to save a talented student like me from demoralizing, my father paid donation in that top college where my friends have taken admission. I tried forgetting that incident& feeling of injustice& tried to concentrate in studies, but my negative mentality kept on spoiling my studies and I ended up getting less marks in 12th standard board examination. After that due to my good conceptual clarity, I got admission in Engineering in Mumbai University but not in the best college. Again, my negative thoughts did not leave me and kept haunting me for almost 2 years. I was like just above average student, but then I started reading about NLP techniques while searching about how to forget past painful memories. I also attended some NLP seminars & I started practicing those techniques. I also applied visualization technique to give positive signals to my neurons about future. From third year of Engineering my academic graph started ascending. I did extremely well in my academic projects. I worked in elite organizations such as Mahindra & Mahindra, but due to interest in teaching & training profession, I did my MBA in which I was the University topper in marketing subject & then started my Competitive Exams Training Company – Asha careers in the name of my mother & training company –Shareskills along with Shruti madam & now enjoying 'Bliss' in my life. I just want to say that we should not dwell in our past; it keeps haunting us & affects our present &future. We should erase past painful memories & keep past beautiful moments &learning from the mistakes we did or something wrong which happened with us. **–Vaibhav Vasant Patil**

**TIP FOR DEALING WITH PAST PAINFUL MEMORY**

It is said that happiness multiplies & grief divides itself if we share it. Telling our story helps to reduce impact of our painful memory. Writing a diary or a Journal, writing a book, giving lectures, and presenting workshops where we partially or completely mention our past painful memory can neutralize our painful memories and have a cathartic effect on our life towards emotional recovery. Photographs don't let us get out of our past, vanish or delete them physically as well as from your mind. Drugs make us forget the past by affecting our nervous system, never use them.

**Participants crying, breaking down & releasing their emotions due to past painful memories within 10 minutes with NLP technique by Shruti madam.**

*'Past pains have some positive learning which can bring us gains!'-Shruti Chitlangiya Dhruve*

## CHAPTER 1.3

## EMPOWERING LIMITING BELIEFS

Dear friends, let us ask you a question, 'do you believe in yourselves?'Think about it. Whatever & whoever you are today, is due to your belief system. Our core beliefs are generated mostly in our past, in our childhood & our life keeps revolving around those limiting boundaries.

In our special belief change workshops in public & corporate trainings, when we keep a bed of broken glass pieces of beer bottles and ask our participants to walk on it, no one comes forward except the one who knew & had belief that they can walk on the glass bed. After that, we use some belief change techniques, apart from that we both walk on glass bed with bare feet. Then slowly people come forward and walk on the glass bed. This demonstration has an immense impact &it's amazing to know people's feedback after walking on glass bed with their feet safe! If you want to wish live demonstration of our glass walk activity, you may visit our YouTube channel 'Shareskillsonline'. Don't forget to subscribe & like it& also pressing bell icon for updates!

## WHAT ARE BELIEFS?

Beliefs are generalizations, feelings of certainty on the basis of events or references that we perceive & accept as true. Belief system is the root cause behind joyous life or devastated miserable life. It is beliefs that make some people heroes &some people zeroes. You might believe something based on some past references, facts, opinions or assumptions. Our beliefs are driven by our generalizations about what we have learned or have experienced and could lead us to pain or pleasure. Our belief system is not necessarily correct. Interestingly, we are driven by our beliefs. When we believe in something & repetitively expose our subconscious mind to that belief, we will unconsciously look for evidences, references & experiences that will confirm and reinforce our beliefs as true. **Generally beliefs are formed in early childhood.** E.g. Beliefs about money, education etc. Beliefs guide us towards our success or failures. Generalizations sometimes create limiting beliefs such as 'I am born in poor family', 'I can't become rich', 'and I am wasting my time in preparing for this competition because I always lose'. Another example can be-negative beliefs about money such as, 'People with more money with them are bad people', and they will always keep you away from earning more money. Beliefs have the power to construct & the power to destruct as well. Belief system plays a vital role in healthy recoveries, financial state, good or bad relationships & shaping our careers.

## WHY IS IT IMPORTANT TO CHANGE BELIEFS?

If we can develop a sense of conviction or strong certainty of powerful beliefs, then we can achieve anything including those milestones which we ourselves or some other people have thought **'impossible to achieve'**. We should never feed limiting beliefs to our subconscious self in order to succeed & achieve beyond our limits. Holding & nourishing the limiting beliefs is like injecting poison into our thought process & destroying self-conviction, which can make us die emotionally. It is important to change our limiting beliefs because whatever we believe, our mind does deletion, distortion & generalizations of input references from environment & explore only references to justify those limiting beliefs, regardless of its consequences. Limiting beliefs will never allow us to break shackles of our self-limits of success or achievements & we will always be on the same level or even hit rock bottom stage in our life. Your limiting beliefs keep you away from sailing beyond the comfort of your self-imposed horizons. The more deeply ingrained those beliefs are, the greater their unconscious influence are on your actions, habits and, ultimately, your results.

## HOW TO CHANGE YOUR LIMITING BELIEFS?

All personal positive transformations & achievements commence with a massive change in beliefs. The most effective way to change our limiting beliefs is to associate negativity to it. We should think that this limiting belief has already destroyed our past and is affecting & limiting our present & will similarly rule us in future towards failures & pain. On the other hand, we should make a belief statement which is opposite to the limiting belief which will be empowering belief. (E.g. for negative belief such as, **'I am a failed person'** can be an empowering belief, **'I have the ability to become a successful person'**. Then associate immense happiness to the idea of adopting a new empowering belief. Interestingly, its association of pain works more effectively than association of happiness. Another way to changing your limiting beliefs are **'Raise Questions to Counter Your Limiting Beliefs'**. If you raise questions for yourselves, you will find supporting references, events, and experiences, examples which will counter the limiting beliefs & make way for new empowering beliefs. E.g. in case of your empowering belief, **'I have the ability to become a successful person',** the supporting references can be your past achievements or rewards in any field.

(Image resource: First By Rakicevic Nenad from Pexels & second from Pixabay)

**How a man would have been on moon without having belief that, 'We can do it'?**

**TECHNIQUE TO CHANGE BELIEF**

It is essential to come out of our comfort zone and change our limiting beliefs into empowering beliefs to transform our lives towards betterment & prosperity. The following exercise will initiate the process of belief change and will slowly result into your belief change which will have positive impact in all important aspect of your life.

- Explore any negative or limiting belief you hold about yourself, jobs, money, health, relationships, success, career etc. If you are not getting any such limiting belief, go into your past & explore for such belief. E.g. 'Rich people having abundant money are bad' is negative belief about money; 'I can't look healthy' is negative belief about health etc.

- Now, think of this belief. Use sub modalities and five senses for this limiting beliefs. See pictures; hear sounds and experience feelings related with these limiting beliefs.

- Now think, is this limiting belief a standard universal truth or just your random general opinion? (A universal truth example can be –'The sun rises in the east'). Definitely, this belief is based on some particular reference or event hence it is a random general opinion only and need not be always true and can be changed or modified anytime.

- Now, we will associate pain to this limiting belief. Think that if I keep this random generalized opinion, what are the betterments& pains that I have to endure? Or how this opinion will harm my growth in my life? Use sub-modalities and associate all your five senses to those pictures, sounds and feelings of pains and intensify them. Associate completely.

- Raise some logical, rational questions about limiting beliefs which will attack on foundations of that limiting belief.(Use meta models for better results)
Example, if your limiting belief is,' All rich people are bad', then you can raise questions & think such as, 'All? 'Especially when you will find some rich people around you who are actually good.

- Now, think of one empowering belief which will counter and replace the old limiting belief. Example, if you're limiting belief is, **'Life is a punishment'**. Then its empowering belief can be,' **Life is a gift'**.

- Now, you will explore examples and references in the context of your empowering beliefs which will strengthen it further and prove it true as convincingly as if it is a universal truth.

- Now dilute and change old sub modalities of limiting belief with opposite bold sub modalities of empowering beliefs. For example, make the color of pictures of old limiting beliefs blur and diminish them, make them black & white and replace it with colorful pictures of new empowering beliefs. Lower the sounds of limiting beliefs, slowly mute them and replace them with sounds of empowering beliefs.

- Now, we will associate pleasures to this empowering belief. Think that, if I keep this empowering belief, what are the pleasures and gains I can have? Or how this empowering belief will enhance my growth in life? Use sub modalities and associate your all five senses to those pictures, sounds and feelings of pleasures and gains, intensify them. Associate completely and keep enjoying.

- After enough repetition and visualization, take a notebook and write what actions you can take for excelling in your life or solving existing problems.

Does this exercise in your free time, travelling, before you go to bed or sleep at night and after you wake up in morning? Let this new belief go and sink down deep into your subconscious mind with **consistent repetition.** After a few days you will realize your actions and thought process is changing and you are seeing new avenues& opportunities as your core limiting beliefs have changed and replaced by empowering beliefs

## PERSONAL EXPERIENCE ON BELIEF CHANGE

I strongly believe that we always inculcate the seed of belief from the early childhood & that is where I could sense it later after introspecting my own life when that seed of love, hatred, the feeling of being worth for nothing, my incapability, my intellectual level to zero- all these things took seed in my childhood from where now, I had to remove those beliefs.

I belong to Rajasthan and was born & grew up there. Being from Marwari family, I remember that, the girl child used to be unwelcome child and to add on to my negativity, my father had lost his job at very early stage, probably the time when my mother gave birth to me. They had to leave me in joint family at a very early stage of the life, as he never wanted to compromise with my studies. That's why he had left me in Rajasthan. I will not blame anyone for anything but I'll say coming out of that scenario, I always used to crave for love of my parents, my siblings, my family members. I always wanted love in my life. I remember, because of all these things I could never focus in my studies. One of my relatives ended up quoting with entire conviction that," I bet that this girl will not be able to pass even her tenth standard exam". My belief became-I am a loser and no one loves me, am not meant for love as I always got criticism. I always ended up proving people that I am not guilty, I am able, and I am innocent. But, I am happy for what my relative conveyed such damaging lines to me at that time. It hammered me so much that it had actually entered in my strong belief system that firstly- I am good for nothing because no one loves me. Nobody needs me. Secondly I am a duffer - I am not at all capable to complete even my 10th standard. Everything started hammering me so badly in my life. I could see myself growing in same state of mind but thankfully I can say now I am a completely different person & this I would say thanks to all my studies. At the right time, I could change my beliefs, Today if I turn back, I'll definitely say thanks to my cousin and to all my family members who taught me how to overcome such situation. Today I can say that my son who is growing up with me knows only one thing that is my mother is the best and she is the strongest women he has ever met. He doesn't know anything of my childhood & I never want to let him know anything about it because this is what reality is. Today I know and I have learnt how to love my own self, you should know how to love your own self and this will change the entire word around you.

Now my new belief says, 'love is not to be found in outside world but to be found from within'. I also inculcated an empowering belief into me that, 'I am able ','I am enough'.

I started focusing my attention on myself, my health, my career and my goals in life. I started loving myself and caring myself. My beliefs changed completely from 'I am never loved', 'I need love' to ' I love myself ', ' Love for self lies within' .I became a self-reliant person. I was no more dependent on others to love me but after applying belief change techniques I could change my limiting belief towards empowering belief. My belief also changed from, 'I am a loser' to 'I am brilliant & a highly intellectual' person. Today, I am achieving great heights in transforming lives of people & students. All get attached with me& become close to me. Friends! It is possible only because I could change my limiting beliefs at the right time.

-**Shruti Chitlangia Dhruve**

**BELIEF CHANGE IN GYM**

As a corporate/public trainer or coach it is important to take care of your physical fitness as you are the center of attraction of people during public & corporate workshops. The only intention of my joining the gym was to keep my body & mind active. I was not much interested on lifting more weights during weight training. But once my trainer told me that my body is showing amazing results even when I am not using many weights, so if I increase weights then it will show even better results. So I decided to lift more weights, where I faced problems due to my limiting beliefs. I used to see some specific numbers in weights and beyond those numbers my belief was I would not be able to lift those weights & I would have ended up doing my workout sets with wrong forms &techniques, or even experienced minor muscle injuries.

Then I decided to apply belief change techniques. I started writing down my limiting beliefs & started associating pain with them & then converted those limiting beliefs into empowering beliefs & started visualizing with those new empowering beliefs. I also invented one smart effective experiment to make myself able to lift more weights. I started closing my eyes while lifting weights. I asked my trainer to put more weights than my regular weights. I stopped counting repetitions of sets & used to utilize my potential to maximum. I also used to think about my idols such as Salman Khan, Arnold Schwarzenegger etc. & execute some **modeling excellence techniques**(we do it in advance NLP course & will be also including in advance NLP series of - The Bliss) while doing workouts. To my surprise after one week my gym trainer said that now I could lift almost double the weights I used to lift one week ago.

I always took care that I never saw how much weights I am lifting during this transition period, which actually helped me change my limiting beliefs.

-**Vaibhav Vasant Patil**

**TIP FOR CHANGING LIMITING BELIEFS**

Have a look at your list of limiting beliefs, labels (words which other people often use for you such as duffer, fat, ugly, scholarly, smart, and naughty), and thoughts& make a list as one element per piece of paper. Now, create list of empowering beliefs & labels for you from your own perspectives which will counter those limiting beliefs & labels. Make a list on one element per piece of paper. Now, take a cardboard. Paste a big picture of brain on it which will represent your brain. Take a limiting belief, tear it off & keep it aside. Then take an empowering belief which will counter the limiting belief & paste it in the brain area of cardboard. You will realize that a lot of the labels you have kept aside are simply because someone else likes parents, teachers, relatives, friends, and colleagues have said it and you believed it. Those were not your own labels. It didn't matter if it was really true or not, you believed it and you continued to believe it till now. Always remember, you don't have to accept any label that anyone tries to stick to you. So, when you hear someone making a comment like that, just say, "Excuse me, but this does not apply to me."This answer will protect your subconscious mind from external generalized limiting beliefs.

**Trainer & participants walking, jumping on glass bed.**

*'If you believe in yourself, the sky is the limit for your achievements'-Vaibhav Vasant Patil*

# CHAPTER 1.4

## *TRANSFORMING SELF*

Friends, do you know a caterpillar? Have you ever seen it? It's the initial ugly phase which undergoes transformation into a beautiful butterfly. In its caterpillar stage it looks disgusting& can't fly as it doesn't have wings. But, as you might know every caterpillar can undergo self transformation into a butterfly in later stages. For that  the caterpillar has to take care of itself, make itself ready for self transformation, has to eat lot of leaves & sleep a lot ,due to which it forms a cocoon around it, then wings originate ,grow & finally a beautiful butterfly spread its wings and flies high. Every one of us wants to become that beautiful butterfly, capture attention of people, want financial freedom, luxurious lifestyle, prosperity& security in life, but the reality with most people is that they are in a stage of mundane, deficient caterpillar. Of course with power of mind, hard smart work they can reach the stage of the beautiful, pleasant butterfly in their lives but for that they need to undergo a process called as **'Self-Transformation'.**

## WHAT IS SELF TRANSFORMATION?

The caterpillar doesn't get transformed into a butterfly by chance; similarly the personal self transformation doesn't randomly occur. Self-transformation is a process by our own self to form new transitions for holistic wellness in life. Self-transformation doesn't necessarily need to be a big thing or lengthy process but it necessarily needs to be effective enough to originate root of change & escalate towards 360 degree transformation. Self transformation means opening our mind towards something for which **it has been closed since years.** It may consist of **learning a new productive thing or enhancing an old one towards perfection.**

Self transformation sets us free from our limiting beliefs & self-doubts. It replaces fear of failure to confidence& towards success. It inculcates & develops a new winning attitude. It helps us to do things in new innovative ways and in a productive manner. It can be learning from our mistakes & correcting them for betterment. Self transformation can bring us towards a healthy life, bright career, financial freedom, prosperity & self transformed personal as well as professional relations.

## WHY IS SELF TRANSFORMATION NECESSARY?

If we introspect ourselves, we can find many areas where we are lacking & lagging behind which is causing us pain, harm, loss& keeping us off-track from others. It might be our health, poor financial aspects, limiting beliefs, defunct& nagging relations etc. Changing & transforming others is difficult. We can try to motivate, convince or influence others, but at the end of the day, for compatibility with environment, external-internal challenges & to withstand other people, changing &transforming yourself is the fastest way to change our perspectives & final outcome. After all, we are controllers of our attitude and actions. Rather than playing **"the blame game"**, ranting& pointing fingers at others, or just wishing that somebody should have been different, or the situations should have been different, it is always better to focus on self & transform ourselves for betterments. It is obvious that, we get unstuck when we transform ourselves. Our transformation sets us free and leads to our personal powers & success.

(Images Resource: From Pixabay)

**The ugly caterpillar undergoes self transformation to become a beautiful butterfly!**

## HOW TO TRANSFORM SELF?

In reality, many people try to change themselves with willpower but fail because they assume & believe that transformation is lengthy, time consuming, boring &difficult process. They also think transformation is not possible as some things are not in their hands; they also blame time or other such situational factors& external circumstances. Hence accordingly their subconscious mind & neural pathways gets programmed which result in failures. Most of us don't know how to create long lasting change! Also in our culture we find negative associations &barriers towards self transformation where we think about people's perspectives more.

All changes which can lead to transformations can be decided, created & executed in a moment & we should not wait until we are forced to make a shift in our lives by bringing transformation. If we want to change & transform our behavior, habits, patterns, thought process, actions, physical fitness, financial status & quality of relations, then there is an effective way to do it. We should able to link unbearable & quick sensations or feelings of pain to our old behavior & on the other hand motivating, incredible sensations of pleasure to a new one. If we understand how our brain, subconscious & conscious mind works, then we can break our old limiting behavioral & other patterns & if we can simply change what we link happiness & grief to, we can change our nervous system conditioning & transform our old neural pathways to take control of our lives. So, the best tool for long term change & transformation is conditioning. Neuro associative conditioning & NLP are some of the conditioning tools, as our brain whenever experience certain amount of pain or pleasure, it explores for root cause.

## CAREER TIMELINE' TECHNIQUE

There are many timeline techniques in NLP, using visual, auditory and kinesthetic sub modalities. Also; we can bring lot of innovative varieties at deeper level. This exercise can be done while standing, sitting down or while sleeping. We can use these techniques for all other important domains of life such as health, wealth, behavior patterns etc.

- Stand in a relaxed way. Imaging the future before you as an ever-expanding triangle, full of colorful resources and best possibilities. Imagine your past going backside in a triangle. Think for few minutes what kind of future you want & what you might do in your career now to achieve that desired future.

- Imagine yourself far ahead in that future where you have achieved your goal in career. You are living the life that you always wanted. Apply all your senses & see those ideal images, hear appreciations, feel the pride & sense of achievement. Fully associate with the images and take time to intensify & enjoy those feelings.

- Dissociate now. Step outside yourself, move towards your future version and watch your present self from that future version. From this viewpoint, list the five key factors or elements that helped you achieve your desired career & future which you have achieved.

- Move halfway back towards the present self. At this halfway point, what have you done to master those five important success factors? What could you do more to improve upon what you did?

- Now come back to the present. What could you do now to start introducing & implementing those five elements in your life?

- Think about your past, what learning and advices can you take from your past failures & mistakes. List down five key elements.

- Imagine yourself introducing & implementing those five elements from future version & five from past into your present life. Imagine yourself moving ahead now, never looking back towards past failures, overcoming any possible barriers that might get in your way, and picking up & implementing additional resources, until you meet your original outcome.

- Now from the time of having achieved your objective, what one advice & one tip would you give to your present self?

- Start again from the present. Move to the future, this time taking account of the advices& tips you've given yourself.

- Thank your conscious & subconscious mind, for taking the time & cooperating yourself to invest in the planning of your career & future for going through those amazing experiences & learning.

## PERSONAL EXPERIENCE ON SELF TRANSFORMATION

I am brought up in a joint family and my parents had to stay away from me for work purpose. I always faced allegations, criticism, and disrespect from others. Such things started to hold me back from doing something excellent and extraordinary in my academics. I used to start any given work or assignment with enthusiasm and excitement but later lose interest in it.

External critical voices haunted me whenever I tried to excel in any field. Those voices got converted into internal critical voices, affecting me all through my childhood till my college days. Feeling of being alone made me a rebel child, resulting in low school performance during my initial school days made me further emotionally weak, adding no worthy feeling to myself. During my graduation, I started reading and practicing NLP books along with emotional intelligence and slowly started using these techniques to mute my internal critical voices. I started using certain affirmations like- I am stronger, I am healthy, I am worthy. These affirmations helped me to be in a resourceful state. I even prepared vision board and used these techniques. Everything accumulated together to help me mute my inner critical voices. Later, in my college years, I came to know about NLP and Emotional Intelligence through various books and I started executing those techniques. As I practiced those techniques, I gradually cleansed those limitations and demoralizing thoughts which were holding me back from excelling in my career.

My self-transformation majorly includes my improved communication skills, enhanced appearance, strong intellectual level and the most important is my interpersonal skills with people. These evolved combinations helped me transformed completely.

I still remember, my accent, grammar, pronunciation were not up to the mark. My inner confidence was fragmentary, completely shattered as I never got support from anyone saying 'Yes! You can do it' and it was my mistake that I was seeking external help for that kind of motivation. One thing everyone knows is that, if you are not good in communication, you will never feel confident while talking with others. I used to feel ashamed of my own self because of my poor communication skills and the people around me further added negative vibes that I am truly not worthy of anything. Talking about my looks, I was a tall child who appeared malnourished with dark complexion. My internal thoughts and feelings made me feel ashamed of my appearance. My relatives disowned me. Thankfully I have come over all these things and with entire transformation from my looks to my communication, interpersonal skills, academics-everything is absolutely different and a flip over world now.

This wasn't an overnight change. I still remember the time which I had spent with my father. He taught me things quite closer and similar to NLP during my teenage years. He always said that "do not look into others with an intention to just find faults in them, rather introspect your own self, find where you are going wrong, stop blaming others because you have control over your own self but no control over others. Remember, you can always change yourself but not necessarily the situation around you". With this valuable base, I started reading more books related to NLP and emotional intelligence which only increased my knowledge and understanding on the subject. Those included all the facts and figures, scientific and psychological reasons behind every output. This way I found the purpose of my life.

On the academic front, I completed my CS, MBA and M.COM and started to teach in colleges and various institutions like CA, CS, and ACCA Institutes as a lecturer. I am proud to say that now I am one of the senior faculties in this domain with many awards, accolades and recognitions. I started spreading my knowledge and expertise through training and coaching adding goodwill across various locations in and outside the city - Mumbai Suburbs, Thane, Surat, Vapi, Pune, Navi Mumbai, and Delhi. So here is my strong message to all of you - for self-transformation, first step is to have a strong belief, plan and start to visualize yourself doing and achieving it.

-   **Shruti Chitlangia Dhruve**

## TIPS FOR SELF TRANSFORMATION

- **VISION BOARD TECHNIQUE FOR SELF TRANSFORMATION:**

Vision board technique is on the basis of the law of attraction. In this we create a sacred space that displays what we want to actually transform to & then destiny & this universe brings it to our life. What we focus on gets expanded. When you create a vision board and place it where you see it regularly, you essentially end up doing short visualization exercises for your self-transformation throughout the day. Your vision board should also focus on how you want to use 5 senses & not just on transformations that you want. You'll be amazed at how things just start entering into your life once you set the intention for what you want and how you want to feel.

### HOW TO MAKE VISION BOARD?

It's all up to your creativity & skills. Buy a large white color cardboard, thermocol or notice board .Take magazines & newspapers. Cut pictures of your desires & dreams & make a collage on cardboard. You can select pictures for best health, bright career, good marks in exams, sharp memory, lovely relations, marriage, great personalities, your idols, money notes, awards, gifts, beautiful clothes, cheques with big amounts etc. for the feeling of holistic life wellness in the six important domains of life health, wealth, relations, careers, memory & personality development. Hang the finished collage at your home or your workplace where you see it on regular basis. It will motivate you for self transformation & your conscious & subconscious mind will take necessary actions towards fulfilling it.

**Students doing vision board activity in outbound training program of Shareskills Trainings**

**A workshop on 'self transformation to self empowerment' in women empowerment program in a college, Mumbai.**

*"Learning self transformation starts with unlearning inertia & comfort zone"*

*- Shruti Chitlangia Dhruve*

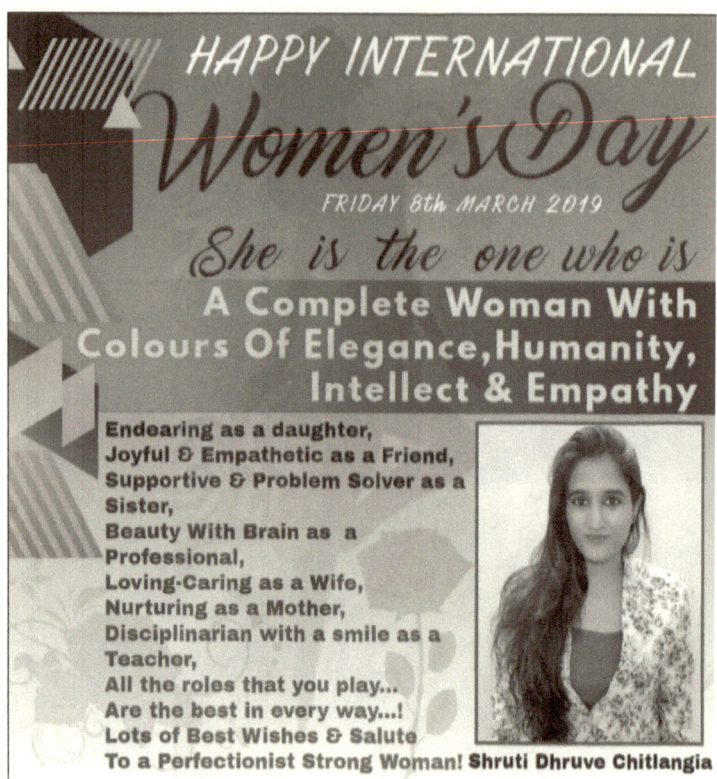

A greeting card made by a student. Self transformation from a girl who was always craving for love, respect, cares & attention to a strong woman who is always showered with abundant respect, appreciations, love & best wishes from all.

*"Learning self transformation starts with unlearning inertia & comfort zone"- Shruti Chitlangia Dhruve*

## *CHAPTER 1.5*

## *ANCHORING*

Have you ever seen a mathematics professor who is also a very sharp memory trainer doing basic calculation mistakes? I, Vaibhav, am myself a very interesting case study. Apart from being an NLP & EI trainer now, I have been the senior most professor for mathematics& aptitude for toughest competitive exams such as UPSC, CAT, CPT, GMAT, IBPS etc. since last 12 years(till 2019) in prestigious colleges &institutes in Mumbai, Pune & other cities. In our introductory workshops I give demo of memorizing 100 digit number created by public on the spot within 3 minutes! Shruti is also highly qualified & teaches in prestigious institutes for B.Com, CA, and CS & ACCA. She is also a memory trainer &proficient in mathematics with extremely good logical & analytical skills. Since the time we met, I always used to feel she is 2 steps ahead of me in terms of smartness. Once we were doing some calculations of our revenues &

expenses after our public training workshop, she asked me a basic calculation of percentage & addition but in hurry with her extreme expressions as always. I fumbled & ended up giving wrong answer. Again, after our next workshop, unintentionally from her, such thing happened couple of times & I ended up giving wrong answers for basic calculations due to hurry or may be due to her extreme expressions made me conscious. But, this audio & visual trigger of questioning by her has become an anchor of myself fumbling or ending up doing calculation errors. Now, after applying anchor collapse techniques, now while doing balance sheet with her, I never get fumble & confidently answer calculations within fraction of seconds even if she asks deliberately at time. Friends, this is nothing but conditioning of mind.

**WHAT IS ANCHORING?**

To understand what is basically anchoring, let's consider one experiment. A Russian scientist Dr. Ivan Pavlov conducted an experiment on dogs. He put some meat in front of dogs at some distance & created a hurdle. Due to that, dogs would see meat but could not eat it. They started salivating & Dr. Pavlov rang the bell. He would show meat to dogs. He repeated this experiment for many days. One day he fed a lot of meat to dogs & they slept & he rang the bell. You will be surprised to know that dogs opened their eyes and started salivating as if they were hungry even they had lot of meat before sleeping. Now whenever he wanted to make dogs salivate, he would ring the bell in absence of meat. The feelings for meat were coming from ringing of bell. This experiment was named as **classical conditioning of mind** where we give same reflexes for same triggers on the basis of five senses. E.g. while driving, whenever we see red light of vehicle in front of us or red light of traffic signal, our foot goes on the brakes which was on the accelerator before that.

(Image resource: ManuelKeusch from Pexels)

**Due to an anchor, the ship remains in a particular zone, similarly our mind gets anchored to a particular state due to triggers or stimuli through our five senses.**

Whenever we are at the peak of any state of mind, that time whenever we see, listen, touch, smell or taste, all these sensors create a link with that state. **The dogs linked audio triggers with hunger; this process of associating our senses with triggers is called as Anchoring.** One or more sensors may get associated with one state. The problem is that, when our state is high on X &at that time if we are sensing thing Y, then we end up creating natural or deliberate Anchor. For example , One day you were in fear suppose due to terror attack in your city& if in this state you see some face, listen music or hear some voice, you will associate a feeling of fear with it. Even if that fear goes, the anchor will recall your fear with the help of sense with which you have created anchor which may remain for long, e.g. the bomb blast incidence in local trains in Mumbai. Some people travelling in local trains relate trigger of local train sound with bomb blast & death of many people which creates a feeling of fear & trauma in them.

From a mental health perspective, a phobia is also a strong example of anchoring where we see, hear or touch something which triggers our fearful emotions.

## WHY YOU SHOULD USE ANCHORS IN LIFE?

You should create positive anchors and remove negative anchors. Anchors are created or can be collapsed deliberately or it may also happen naturally. Imagine you are at the peak of your relation with your spouse or fiancée and at that time you look in each other's eyes; suppose it happened couple of times. Now, whenever you will see in your partner's eyes, you are completely in love. Schools, tuition classes and homes have become bad anchors for children. Suppose couple of times, a student is getting sleepy while studying a specific book. Now, whenever he will read that book again in future, he will feel sleepy, but at the same time if he sits in room where TV is on, then he will not feel sleepy, in fact he will feel fresh. It's more about anchoring rather than deliberate action from that student. We all experience that exams have become anchors of fear, confusion, stomach-ache, migraine for students as well as parents. The problem is student may be learning in a comfortable, resourceful, playful state X like AC room, with good ambience, food, parents accompanying them but in the exam hall there is state Y which is not necessary a resourceful state like X. Creating good anchors helps us lots of times. Anchoring is instant solution & handy tool for our mental & physical problems where apart from good, resourceful anchors there are also some bad anchors created during consumption of alcohol, cigarettes, over-eating etc. If bad anchor is creating problems then we can collapse that anchor. All babas (Godmen) & gurus in India have 5000 years of anchoring. When you see anyone in saffron clothes, beard and tilak on forehead, it means he is baba-a divine soul irrespective of family or academic background of that person. You will respect him/her, you will not ask negative questions, you will touch their feet but if same person comes in formal trousers& shirt then their anchor is defunct. When British came to India, they realized that all people were associated with their kings emotionally. Then they used the dress of raja as dress of their servants, which broke the anchor of kings, as servants used to work under British. We personally feel that our Indian Tricolor-Tiranga should be only used at time of 26 January - Republic day, 15 August –Independence day, events related to police & soldiers, victory days etc. to maintain the aura & dignity of visual anchor of tricolor, but many times we see that tricolor flags are used in home, office tables, sold on footpaths, even sometimes common man's clothes are designed in Tiranga which is diminishing the anchor of tricolor of India. Soldiers always saved their anchors from civilians; they keep themselves isolated from civilians most of the time. Their spine is always straight. They always create& live in their own zone. They have conditioned their bodies and their minds with natural anchoring to kill the enemy and also they are ready to die for nation during wars. Anchoring is more about conditioning of our minds. For instance, one day if you decided with your friends to party hard and you arranged a party and had one peg of alcohol. Then due to the effect of alcohol, you started enjoying more. That created triggers related to drinking &fun and you associated alcohol with pleasure. With anchoring techniques in NLP, you can create anchors for health, wealth, happiness & collapse anchors of past baggage, anxiety, alcohol, smoking, drugs, bad thoughts, & worries. Our Immune system is sensitive; it is getting anchored due to external triggers every time as per psycho-neuro-immunology.

## HOW TO CREATE AN ANCHOR?

We will see one detailed exercise as an example to create anchor of desired state. There are many ways to create, set, test or even collapse an anchor. Just follow below mentioned rules while setting an anchor.

**RULE 1:** We should always gain the desired state **at peak,** anchoring will never get set in half state.

**RULE 2: Anchor should be unique.** E.g. shaking hands cannot become an anchor as in routine life we shake our hands with people in personal or professional lives. You can touch some part of body in unique way and create a kinesthetic anchor. E.g. Red cloth to bull is an example of visual anchor.

**RULE 3: While setting anchor, try it number of times.** It is not necessary that person will go in good state, associate pleasure with desired state or associate disgust or pain with undesirable state in first attempt. Also if you think first attempt is enough, still we will recommend that bring more concentration & consolidation of feelings with repetitions.

**RULE 4:** After setting anchor dissociates, to get the state back use the same anchor and **calibrate** the response of the person's body &feelings. Don't use different anchor for same state. Calibration is getting an accurate idea about persons state by reading & paying close attention to non verbal signals from voice tone and volume, posture, facial color ,eye movements and pupil dilation, muscle tension in the face and forehead , lower lip size breathing pattern.

**HOW TO GAIN STATE?**

You take actions in terms of verbal or nonverbal. Action comes from state and our state comes from events in our mind. Event B is perceived from event A via our five senses. Gaining state at peak, get involved in applying five senses for any desired state you want. Intensify your five senses, then take that state in peak & create an anchor.

You may use your past references to intensify feelings if you are not able to apply five senses for your desired state. For Example In childhood, you have lived a healthy life. Go into the time when you were very healthy. There were many moments when you were very healthy. See what you saw, feel what you used to perform physically. These events are running in your mental screens. As if you are there in those moments. Make them panoramic. Slowly listen to the voices; you are living those moments. With those voices, your states are getting generated. There is difference in your chest, breathings, keeps associating with visuals and sound. With colors you recognize it easily; you are seeing that you are bathing in that color, inhaling those colors. These feelings are increasing and set your anchor. Enjoy the same color. Your body is enjoying the same wellness. Remember last three digits of your telephone number to dissociate. Apply the same technique to derive desired state of playfulness, happiness, the feeling of being loved from other people, feeling of confidence etc.

## ANCHORING DESIRED STATE

This technique will create and hold on to the state of mind which is positive and resourceful. The positive and resourceful state is always important in producing efficient results. This anchoring technique will enable you to utilize positive, enabling resources such as confidence, conviction, joyfulness, perfection, energy, enthusiasm, healthiness etc. and remove negative resources such as negative feelings & thoughts etc. Follow the steps and enjoy resourceful state:

- Choose a place where there is no disturbance
- Think about a state or feeling that you want to gain at your will. For example, for facing an interview, you might require state of confidence and presence of mind which you can obtain with this technique. Let's do this technique for gaining state of confidence.
- Understand how to create an anchor explained above, and choose your anchor as touching your left chest where the heart lies with your right hand.
- Now, think about the present or past, where you have felt confident about yourself. For example, you may have experienced confidence when you were in school or college after getting good marks or rewards. In your office, you might have got promotion or rewards from your boss. Think of any situation where you're feeling of 'confidence' was at its peak level.
- Get completely associated with that situation and event. Experience those events on your mental screen. See the pictures of yourself as a confident person after achieving good things or results in your life. Hear the sounds of appreciation from others, hear internal sounds such as, 'I have done this successfully', 'I am great', 'I am very confident',' Experience the feelings of achievement

and confidence'. Make your body language like a confident person with expressions of confidence on face, chest and shoulder etc. Experience feelings with all your five senses. Enhance sub modalities by making pictures brighter, bolder, more colorful, making sounds louder & by making your feelings more realistic. Repeat this process consistently with more intensity & when you will feel that you are at peak level of your feelings or state of confidence then set an anchor by touching your left chest portion with right hand which is called **firing the anchor.**

- Repeat this process several times till your neurons associates your anchor with your feeling of confidence.

- Now, dissociate from your current state. Speak your mobile number in reverse way, see around and dissociate from this state completely.

- Now test your anchor. Touch left side of your chest with right hand. Are you getting feeling of full of confidence?

- If you are not getting feelings of confidence after firing your anchor, then it's time to reset the anchor. Repeat all the above steps and this time use more intense sub modalities with more brighter, closer pictures, louder sounds with exact words and sentences etc. and with more realistic feelings. Ensure that you are setting the anchor when your feelings are at peak.

- Again test your anchor till it passes the test when fired.
- Now as your anchor is set, you can access this feeling of 'confidence' whenever you require by just firing your anchor. Ensure you regularly practice this process. Also whenever you feel confident naturally, those times don't forget to fire your anchor for its consolidation.
- Congratulate and say thank you to your body, conscious and subconscious mind for cooperating in setting the anchor.

**HOW TO COLLAPSE THE ANCHOR?**

For collapsing any negative, unwanted states of mind or habits, we associate those things with an anchor of disgust, pain etc. For collapsing a bad anchor, we need to create good anchor which counters the bad anchor. Suppose you want to create anchor of healthiness and collapse anchor of illness or anxiety.

Then remember anytime when you were healthy, young and energetic. Go into that time and see, feel, hear those pictures & sounds of healthiness. Imagine a color for those feelings. Let this color of health spread throughout your body & cells. Hear the sounds such as 'I am healthy',' I am energetic' and 'I am young'. Create one unique anchor. Test the anchor. Do it 5 to 10 times.

Now think of your illness or health related anxiety. Imagine a color for this illness. Let the color be bad color.

You don't have to think about negative feelings much as you want to remove them from your mind. Create another unique anchor. Now, you have two anchors. Make sure, if you are pressing respective anchors, the mind will take same feelings. If you press both anchors at same time, then mind will get confused. Colors are mixing and a color of confusion is formed. Let this color flow throughout your body. Now, leave the anchor of illness and continue firing anchor of good health. Collapsing anchor doesn't take time. Anchors make or break brands. For example, the famous cricketer & hero of India's world cup victory Yuvraj Singh, was removed as brand ambassador of REVITAL supplements once he was diagnosed with cancer. Anchoring earns money over endorsements. Celebrities won't appear in casual dressing in public. Their reputation depends as anchor. Their aura has money that's why you can see many celebrities are invisible during their illness as they do not prefer to come in public in that low phase.

**PERSONAL EXPERIENCE ON ANCHORING**

Since childhood I was very fond of bakery products such as sweet bun, bread, toast, butter, biscuits, toast etc, but once from Shruti, I came to know that most of bakery products contains 'processed wheat(Maida in Hindi) &gluten' which is very unhealthy & clogs our arteries & veins which results into high blood pressure & relevant diseases. My consumption of bakery products was very high; you may say I was addicted to freshly baked, hot bakery products. So, problem was that how will I get rid of my habit of bakery products? I tried most of NLP techniques but all of them failed. Then once while reading a book of a famous author, I came across some anchoring techniques to associate & dissociate pain & pleasure by using anchors. Within a few minutes after glancing through techniques, I was confident that if I could modify this technique then I can get rid of not only bakery products but also any other thing which I don't want in my life due to its bad effects. I designed the technique along with Shruti and made it as simple as I could where within few minutes we could get rid of anyone's any unwanted habit which we started using in our two days workshops. Talking about my bakery product habits, after applying anchoring technique designed by us, I could get rid of bakery products completely within one week. Now, even if anyone invite me to taste mouthwatering ,hot bakery products  in any five star hotel for free, I will feel so disgusted that I will pay that person and will ask not to talk about bakery products in front of me.

## ON THE SPOT VOMITING!

The NLP Anchoring technique designed by us is extremely effective & creates wonder during our workshops. We randomly invite any person and ask him/her the thing which they want to get rid of. For effectiveness and to show interesting demonstration to our participants in public, we emphasize to tell any unwanted eating or drinking habit of that person. Then as soon as they tell it, I or Shruti ask them to close their eyes &then execute our NLP Anchoring Technique; it happens that the person ends up vomiting due to nauseated feelings which we associate with the thing from which he or she wants to get rid of. **Most of times**, it is seen that the person vomits on stage or run towards wash basin. After getting to know the high impact of this technique, we started keeping a small bucket near the person who comes on stage.

ANCHORING TIPS

- **MAKE YOUR MEDICINES AS AN ANCHOR OF WELLNESS!** :

You can use anchoring & condition your mind in healthy way while eating medicines. When you eat medicine, many people generally say, **'I am having medicine as I am ill'**. Instead of this, chunk down language and say to self that, **'I am becoming healthy, and that's why I am having this medicine'**. With this you are creating anchor of wellness with that specific medicine or tablet. You can keep medicines in your home temple near God to create **'Placebo Effect'** in medicine. That's why in old times, any natural Ayurveda medicine was associated with God's blessings.

- **MAKE YOUR DRESS AS YOUR ANCHOR OF HAPPINESS!**

We would also like to disclose one of the secrets about our dressing sense. Whenever we are happy after a good training program, after cracking a deal, after designing excellent NLP techniques, when we get some good news, we wear a new dress with some pleasant colors and designs (we continue this for couple of times when we were extremely happy.) We take care not to repeat that dress for any other instance. Now, it happens that whenever we wear that dress, we get feeling of happiness even if no happy moment is around.

- **ANCHOR YOUR OWN FACE!**

This is very interesting & simple technique with best impact in morning, after your bath & morning rituals, you stand in front of mirror. Make sure you have groomed yourself properly before standing in front of the mirror. Now, close your eyes. Go in the past when you have got the feeling of worthiness &confidence, feeling of being loved. Imagine that feeling is coming towards you in the form of colorful clouds and rain on your body. Your body is absorbing that pleasant, blissful rainwater. This rainwater is washing your worries, feelings of illness, your resentments. The feeling of joyfulness, feeling of healthiness is running throughout your body in the form of colors. Create inner voices such as –'**I am healthy & a worthy child of this universe'.** Visualize beautiful images of yourself with wonderful future. Create feelings & sounds that you love yourself. Now, whenever you will feel that you are at peak of your good feelings, then open your eyes & see your face in the mirror. Do it daily in the morning. After some weeks you will realize that whenever you see your face in the mirror you are getting all those wonderful feelings.

- **MAKE YOUR BEDROOM OR BREAKFAST TABLE AS ANCHOR OF JOY, LOVE, and PLAYFULNESS& TOGETHERNESS!**

It is applicable for all married as well as unmarried people. Unmarried, single people can practice it with their family members, siblings or friends. In the morning, when you are with your spouse on bedroom or on breakfast table, play the game of jokes. Keep some jokes ready on paper or in your mobile. Now, tell those jokes to your partner or family members without seeing in the mobile or paper. Keep some small incentive for the person who does it better for that day. Continue this for couple of weeks. You will realize that your bedroom or breakfast table has become anchor of love, joyfulness, smile & togetherness. Couples should never ever fight in bedrooms; else the ugly danger is that the bedroom might become the anchor of fighting& blame games.

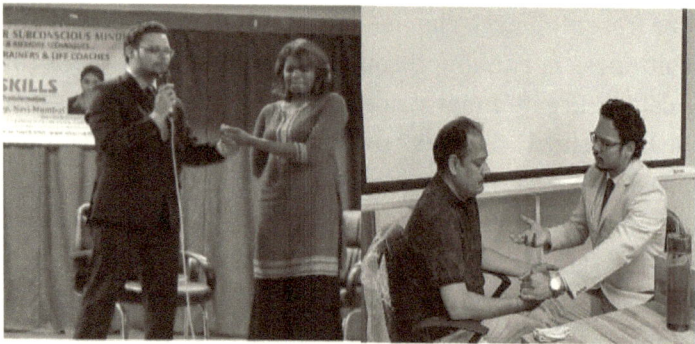

**Participant's intense expressions are visible in live anchor collapse demo in public workshops.**

*PART 2*

*THE BLISS*

*WITH*

*EMOTIONAL INTELLIGENCE*

## CHAPTER 2.1

## INTRODUCTION TO EMOTIONAL INTELLIGENCE

Have you ever experienced emotional blackmailing in your life? You may have been the perpetrator or the victim. Have you controlled others been controlled by others emotionally? Friends, we are human beings and not animals. Emotions are bound to play a big role in our lives. Rather, we will say emotions play the biggest role in our ascent or descent in life. So, it is not a crime if someone manipulates you emotionally, even innocent children try emotional blackmailing techniques on their parents for their demands, but the rational thinking should be always given higher priority than emotional thinking. Rational thinking keeps us in a balanced state & protects ourselves from becoming emotionally drained. As per the report of World Health Organization (WHO) on their website, almost 8, 00,000 people commit suicide every year, which comes out to be one person every 40 seconds worldwide. Going into more depth of this report, we found that suicide occurs in every age group and it is the second leading cause of death among 15-29 year olds globally. The reasons of suicide had specific patterns as per the age groups. Why do you think people commit suicide? One fine day, we got hooked up to the news on TV about SSC board results announcement. Apart from pass or fail our attention was straight away drawn up to the suicide news that was flashing on the news channel. We were shocked to learn the number of students who could not make it to the passing line had committed suicide, but further depressing was the case of few students who had actually passed but still took the tragic step of give up their life even before the results were announced. Stunned by this news, we did not even have lunch that day. It was indeed traumatic for everyone alike.

Who was responsible for their suicide? Parents? Education system? Or they themselves were to be blamed, who were still adolescents? Friends, we started analyzing about it & came to the conclusion that the root cause lies in event A & event B -concepts which we have discussed in NLP section. So many students, almost 16 lakhs, have given the examination; 4 lakh students failed which was considerably a higher number. Then why only that single digit number of students committed suicide & specially those who passed? People committing suicide distort the events; they give some worse meaning to whatever happens with them which results in phobia, anxiety & damaging their self-image. Had they been given a single hour counseling session during their school studies; they would have been alive today. The fault does not lie with the system. The board gives many chances to students for re-examination, but the problem here is that students are not able to cope up with failure& belief system (refer NLP Section Chapter 1) they have created about failures. Even if you survey in corporate or government offices, organizations are in need of 'Emotionally Intelligent' candidates rather than just 'Intelligent' candidates for jobs.

'Emotional Intelligence' has become the need of the hour, especially if you need to excel in your personal & professional life. According to a study by Leadership IQ, 46% of newly-hired employees will fail within 18 months, while only 19% will achieve unequivocal success. But contrary to popular belief, technical skills are not the primary reason why new hires fail; instead, poor interpersonal skills & lack of emotional intelligence dominate the list.

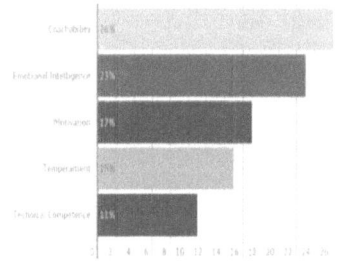

(Image source: www.leadershipiq.com)

**In previous comparative bar graph, you can see top areas of failure & the percentage of respondents.**

The study found that 26% of new hires fail because they can't accept feedback, 23% because they're unable to understand and manage emotions, 17% because they lack the necessary motivation to excel, 15% because they have the wrong temperament for the job, and only 11% failed because they lack the necessary technical skills.

## WHAT IS EMOTIONAL INTELLIGENCE?

When we bring our emotions & intelligence together it is emotional intelligence which is the ability of awareness, control and expression of one's emotions, and to handle interpersonal relationships with empathy. Emotional Intelligence is the ability to recognize, understand and manage our own emotions& also to understand, recognize, manage and influence the emotions of others.

(Image source: By pngtree.com)

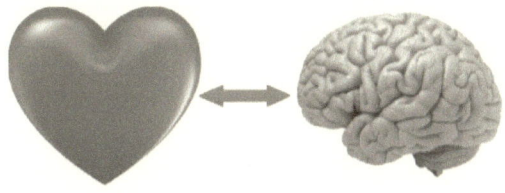

**EI is all about balancing your brain & heart to take rational decisions for yourself & others.**

EI simply means being aware of each other's emotions which can drive and influence each other's behavior and it is learning about how to manage those emotions especially when we are under influence of certain emotionally susceptible critical situations. It understands how those emotions control our thought process and actions so we can have greater control over our behavior and enhances the skills to manage ourselves more effectively. It allows us to grow and gain a deeper understanding of what we are, enabling us to communicate better with others and build stronger relationships.

## GOLEMAN'S MODEL OF EMOTIONAL INTELLIGENCE:

This model is the most accepted & used model in Emotional Intelligence trainings &content. It consists of four parameters.

- **Knowing Self:** Understanding & becoming completely aware of emotions of self & impact of those emotions on self & others.
- **Managing Self:** It is about managing, monitoring, controlling& directing our emotions before they can cause harm to us or others.
- **Motivation:** It is about utilizing energy of our emotions to achieve our goals.
- **Empathy:** It is thinking from others' perspective, understand; get judgment of others' emotions to take better course of action with them.

- **Interpersonal skills Or Social Skills:** It manages relationships with others.

  So, Emotional Intelligence is all about becoming aware of & managing these five domains in our life for overall emotional wellness of ourselves & others. We need to ensure while implementing Emotional Intelligence, the above parameters are kept at center stage.

## 'I AM THE SUN' TECHNIQUE

It is a useful technique to accept allegations & criticism without allowing ourselves or others bring you down. This technique can be used to accept criticism without letting yourself down. In this technique, we act like a powerful sun that keeps absorbing things. Imagine you are the sun. When someone throws some criticism, allegations and opinions at you, you absorb those things without throwing them back to people and arguing. This is a very simple and effective technique to use against people who keep criticizing& taunting you repeatedly.

Examples: Suppose someone accuses you like this:

**"You are just stupid"**

**"You are lazy only"**

**"You are careless"**

**"You are irresponsible"**

You should simply accept the criticism, true or not, and then repeat it back to the person who criticized you in a calm & composed way.

**"Yes, I am just stupid"**

**"Yes, I am lazy only"**

**"Yes, I am careless"**

**"Yes, I just don't take responsibility"**

Keep doing this to the people who are throwing the stones of allegations at you, and you will realize eventually people making allegations on you, will tone down or stop doing it.. This is an easy and effective method to avoid a back and forth argument and just let the other person's anger & resentment flow out of him. Practice this with someone you know well, by telling them to criticize you rapidly and follow this technique and see how it feels. Use it wisely and in appropriate circumstances. We can also use point of view technique (Refer chapter Empathetic Thinking) to understand why that person is behaving & talking like this way and if he or she has some past baggage?

**WHY EI IS IMPORTANT?**

Emotional intelligence emphasizes on not to get affected & disturbed by **inevitable external events** which are painful, frustrating and may stagnate & impact negatively to our personal or professional life. Emotional Intelligence works as a protective **shield from negative** people or situations. According to a survey by WHO, almost 80% of our personal & professional success depends upon emotional intelligence; hence it is very important to spend time on it. In professional life we can outsource everything- technical skills, software etc, but we can't outsource relationship building, emotional intelligence or emotional challenges faced by us or our team members. Lot of people are good in IQ(Intelligence Quotient) but still they are not able to give their best in professional or personal life, but on the other hand lots of people have low IQ, but with the help of enhanced emotional intelligence, they excel in not only professional but also personal life.

**HOW TO IMPROVE EMOTIONAL INTELLIGENCE?**

To a large extent, our emotional intelligence starts in childhood with how we are raised, but as adults, we can take responsibility to become emotionally intelligent. It's not possible for everyone to consult a personal psychotherapist but we can become our own therapist. Important process in this is learning how to get **awareness of our feelings**. Developing the ability to tune into our own emotions is the first and perhaps most important step. **Self-awareness is the key** behind applying emotional intelligence in our daily life. First connect with your own emotions then we can connect with emotions of others in better way. Use this awareness to manage ourselves & then manage our relations. When we are more aware of our emotions and typical reactions, then we can start to control them in an intelligent way. While dealing with emotional intelligence, we need to be more empathetic by understanding the "Why" factor. Try to understand the "why" behind another person's behavior, feelings or emotions. While handling criticism by others, find positive intention behind criticism & learn from it rather than defending our behavior or mistakes. Our emotions and relevant behavior comes from within us & not from anyone else and once **we start accepting responsibility for how we feel and how we behave,** it will have a positive impact on all areas of our life. Try to explore links between your feelings and also explore the past& find the times you have felt the same way. When tough or extreme feeling arises, ask yourself, "When have I faced this before?" It may help you to realize if our present emotional state is reflective of the current situation or of some other past event.

## AFFIRMATIONS METHOD FOR SIX IMPORTANT DOMAINS OF LIFE:

Affirmations give positive vibes to our subconscious mind. Our thought process usually consists of a mixture of words, sentences, mental images, feelings and sensations. It is essential to be careful of what goes into our subconscious mind. If words and thoughts are repeated, they often get intense & stronger by consistent repetitions, sink into our subconscious mind and govern our behavior, actions and reactions of the person or situations involved. The subconscious mind takes the words and thoughts that get lodged inside it, as if a real situation, and therefore align the words and thoughts with reality. For example, if you repeatedly tell yourself that it is impossible to acquire abundant money then the subconscious mind will accept your words and put barriers in your way but on the other hand, if you keep consistently telling yourself that you are rich or becoming rich, it will find ways to bring you opportunities to get you rich and push you towards taking advantage of these opportunities. Affirmations for six important domains of life are mentioned below. Consistently recite them at the time of sleeping and after you wake up. You can also repeat them whenever you are travelling, having food or driving. You can make audios to hear & recite them regularly such as alarm tunes, mobile ring tones etc.

## 1) HEALTH

I am healthy child of this universe

I have total control on my diet

I love myself and I am perfectly healthy.

Every cell in my body is healthy. I am a health maniac.

My body has immense immune power & healing capacity.

Every day is a new day full of hopes, happiness and health.

## 2) WEALTH

Wealth floats around me daily.

Every day I am becoming richer and richer.

Money comes to me easily and effortlessly.

Wealth constantly flows into my life.

I am living in abundance.

I am a magnet for money.

## 3) RELATIONS

My inner child receives my love daily.

I am getting shower of love from my relations.

My heart is always open to accept people.

All my relationships are long lasting and loving.

I & my life partner are in best harmony.

I& my life partner unconditionally love each other.

## 4) CAREER

I am & always will be enough.

I believe in my abilities to excel in career.

I am giving my best to achieve the best.

I have the power to create a bright career.

I have all needed resources to make a successful career. I am surrounded by positive & supportive people who believe in me.

## 5) MEMORY

I recall any information quickly.

I have a clear mind.

I have a reliable memory.

I can easily concentrate.

I am strengthening my memory.

I am accurately remembering things.

## 6) PERSONALITY DEVELIOPEMENT

I am full of positive energy & confidence.

I always lead the conversation & discussions.

I love being the center of attraction in the parties.

I am becoming the best communicator & public speaker.

I enjoy hearing my own voice.

I am becoming confident & successful.

## EMOTIONAL INTELLIGENCE; PERSONAL EXPERIENCE

We have been invited by the Maharashtra Government Forest Department's Forest Guards Training Center by the Director of Govt. Forest Training Institute, Shahapur, District-Thane on programming their mind for the tough job in jungle apart from emotional intelligence training.

In ice breaking session with those forest trainees, we came to know that they are undergoing rigorous training from morning to evening with very little breaks for breakfast and lunch in between. It was summer and many trainees especially female trainees said that they are finding it very much difficult to cope up with the training and tight schedule. Apart from trainees, there were some senior level forest officers and employees. The problem for them was almost the same, but they were used to that tough & hectic job as they were working in forest department since many years. Still they said 24 hours duty, jungle fires, animal entry into civil areas were some of their major emotionally draining problems. Another issue was although they were giving their 100%, the normal civilians were not giving them appreciation. Now, we got the reason why we were invited.

It was a good ice breaking session as we came to know the exact problems. It was important to prepare them emotionally rather than physically.

We first trained them how to get aware of their emotions. Then we did an activity on how to fully live in present without dwelling about the past and without worrying about the future. Then we took them through visualization techniques, where we associated pleasures to their lives when they will do well in their forest job such as awards and recognitions, financial stability, benefits & facilities they will be getting as Government Employees etc. Then after these core NLP & EI exercises we did, change their state of mind with a laughter therapy. Many of them were smiling as if they were smiling for the first time; they even agreed after session that they enjoyed laughing after a long time. Many female participants mentioned about their mood swings and asked for any solution. We taught them about planning their moods in advance with a slot of 2 hours each. The idea seemed striking to them which was visible from their convincing smiles.

Some forest employees mentioned about their health hazards due to working in core forest areas on which we did musical rainbow fish technique(Refer NLP Chapter 1). Many were extremely happy and satisfied with the pleasant & convincing feeling they got with rainbow fish technique. We ended session with national anthem, group photos and selfies. Many participants often call now and give amazing feedback about how NLP & EI have changed their lives in the forest! We both feel extremely lucky and satisfied when we are showered with love, respect and blessings from our participants who tell that it's only because of us that their lives have been transformed. NLP&EI is indeed a blessing for us.

**NLP & EI training to Maharashtra Forest Department employees & trainees, Shahapur, Thane**

**Photos are visual anchors which trigger our memories & emotions of that event**

**The memento moment!     The gesture of Shareskills!**

## TIP ON EMOTIONAL INTELLIGENCE

Celebrate the positive moments & emotions of everyone. Celebrating and capitalizing on every positive moment in life is essential to keep our mind rejuvenated and resourceful. When we deliberately experience positive emotions, we give positive signals to our neurons which get **reflected in positive things in our personal & professional life.** When we radiate positive & happy vibrations, we attract positive people & situations. Celebrations secrete happy hormones which is good for our emotional & physical health.

If we celebrate happiness & positive emotions with self or others, we are generally more likely to have better relationships with them. So, celebrate holidays, success of your friends or colleagues, your 1st day at new job, celebrate exam results, all festivals, marriages of your friends, relatives and marriage anniversaries of your parents etc.

I will suggest celebrating failures too. Failures can be in your academics, professional or personal life. Here you need to find at least one positive intention & one learning behind your failure. While celebrating failures, you need to remember the theme, intention and use affirmations such as,' I am improving', 'I am becoming ready for success' etc. Celebrations make us aware of our emotions and are important for managing and controlling them.

First I used to think that diverse celebrations & festivals in India are a waste of time and loss for some businesses due to holidays and shut downs but now I think there is a genuine & rational reason behind all celebrations and festivals which is nothing but 'overall wellness in the life of people.'

> *"Emotional Intelligence is the consequence of best balance between heart & brain!"*
>
> *-Shruti Chitlangia Dhruve*

## CHAPTER 2.2

## THINKING EMPATHETICALLY

How much do you support the concept of **'Generation Gap?'** You all must have had some severe arguments with parents, spouse, friends or relatives in your life at least once? Most of us might have concluded that it is generation gap in case of arguments with parents! Parents cannot understand our generation, their thinking is outdated, and they are old fashioned. Friends, you always need to think about positive intention behind every event which happens with you! Question which we want to raise here is not about generation gap, but have you ever put yourselves in the parents' place and thought from their point of view? If you even think for 1 minute about any argument you had with parents, you will realize it was their unconditional love, cares, good thoughts about your future or you will also realize that there might be other reasons such as lack of resources with your parents due to their financial conditions or may be its their past baggage in life. Never think that the person is wrong or become judgmental about person because there must be some reason behind the behavior of the person. E.g. a person might be lacking in money, love from others, self confidence etc or might be having other loads of responsibilities and that's why the person may be facing issues in current life.

This activity related to parents is one of the activities which we do in our emotional intelligence workshops where many people end up crying and calling their parents to say sorry. Empathetic thinking is a skill and if you want cordial, never ending, ever green, harmonious personal or professional relations then **empathy is a boon** for you!

**WHAT IS EMPATHETIC THINKING?**

Empathetic thinking is thinking from point of view of others to 'relate' in relationship with them. What are 6 from my point of view will be 9 from other person's point of view. What is 'Concave' from my point of view, is 'Convex' from others point of view. **Empathetic thinking means "trying to understand others instead of expecting to be understood by others"! Empathy is "walking a road of relationships by putting oneself into the other's shoes"** for mutual understanding & long term, win-win harmony in relationship. Mirror neurons have reshaped the way we can think about how human relate to each other in relationship. This empathetic thinking is essential strategy behind rapport building which is very helpful in personal & professional relationships.

## WHY EMPATHETIC THINKING IS NECESSARY?

Many times in most of the fights in relationships, it happens that people involved in fights are unable to put themselves at other persons place & look at the conflicting situation from other's perspective. In most of the fights, nobody is right or wrong, but still each person tries to force things from his/her perspectives on other which is origin of famous **'Blame Game'**. Healthy & harmonious relationship is the most important pillar of happiness in any human life. If we are not happy in our relations, then all other achievements are in vain & on the other hand if we are happy & fully satisfied in our relationships, then even after all failures we can celebrate together.

## HOW TO THINK EMPATHETICALLY?

Perceptual positions is a form of empathetic thinking that allows us to step into someone else's shoes and see what they see, hear what they hear, and feel what they feel. Perceptual positions help us get a much better impression of the other's or clients **'real possible mind'**. This is because when we imagine we're sitting or standing as someone else, in their posture, speaking with their voice, breathing in their pattern, we pick up a lot of information about what they're thinking and how they are feeling. This process makes it possible for us to improve our interpersonal skills by seeing (and hearing and feeling) things from someone else's perspective. Understanding other's point of view is important for empathetic thinking. It requires soft communication & deeper conversations. We should first become a good listener & listen more than we speak & ask relevant questions as a response to other person's communication with us. Hence, whenever communicating with the person with whom you want to explore & improvise relation, always express your perspectives first. Begin by first sharing your own experiences and perspectives and see if that other person follows the suit. Try to build rapport with that person with **Matching & Mirroring techniques** (Refer rapport building chapter). Use name of that person while communicating for better rapport, smiling, encouraging them, listening to them without interrupting. This type of conversation will lay the strong foundation for a better professional or personal relationship & empathic thinking with the person. Communication & rapport building is the essential step towards empathetic thinking. Healthy & harmonious relationships are most important pillars of happiness in any human life. If we are not happy in our relations, then all other achievements are in vain. Perceptual positions is a form of empathetic thinking technique that allows us to step into somebody else's shoes (position) and see what they see, hear what they hear and feel what they feel. Perceptual positions help us to get a much better impression of the client's **'real possible mind'**. This is because when we imagine we are sitting or standing as someone else, in their posture, speaking with their voice, we pick up a lot of information about their thinking and feelings. Mirroring other person's positions awakens our mirror neurons for better understanding of others. This process makes it possible for us to improve our interpersonal skills by seeing (and hearing and feeling) things from someone else's perspective. There are **four positions** that we can adopt to fully understand other's point of view. These positions are:

• **1ST POSITION:** is fixed position where we are associated with ourselves and we see things from our own fixed point of view.

• **2ND POSITION:** is empathy position where we dissociate from ourselves and imagine we are in someone else's body. We see things from their point of view. You can feel other person's feelings.

• **3RD POSITION:** is observer where we're an independent, neutral observer can watch & assess the interaction between people at positions 1 and 2. We see things from an outsider's point of view.

• **4TH POSITION:** is observing people at 3rd position which relates to their advices, solutions, suggestions & rethinks on it. Imagine some gods; godly people, big leaders are sitting with you at this position and discussing advices & suggestions of people at 3rd position.

**'POINT OF VIEW'TECHNIQUE TO EXPLORE & IMPROVE ANY PERSONAL OR PROFESSIONAL RELATIONSHIP:**

There is point of view to 'relate' in relationship. What will 6 be from one person's point of view will be 9 from other person's point of view. What is beautiful from one person's point of view may be ugly from other person's point of view. We also see that for same event, different person have different views & perspectives. Why it always happens that no one wins in any argument? It is because the people doing arguments lack empathetic thinking for others. Think of a person with whom you want to explore the relation. Let's take a technique to explore our relationships. **Meaning of your communication is the response you get,** means, if you want to change response from other person, then you need to change your communication with that person. Change it till you get desired result. It's our responsibility. You can use it with your family, client, spouse etc. Problem in relationships is that either dominating position 1 or position 2.

(**Image source:** Image by Tumisu from Pixabay)

**What is 'Concave' from one person's perspective may be 'Convex' from other person's perspective.**

Our life will be better when we will become a better balanced observer at position 3 & 4. Let's say that you want to improve relationship with any one important person in professional or personal life. Follow these steps:

- Sit in a chair. Imagine yourself in 1st position. Imagine a 1minute movie of the interaction between you and the other person from your perspective. Ask interrogative questions such as, 'How good or bad this relationship is?', and 'What is the quality of this relation? 'What is making this relation bitter?' .Now write down all the analysis about this relation. Dissociate from situation. Look around & sit at other chair.

- Now, imagine yourself as the other person in the 2nd position, then replay the movie as if, you have entered into other person's body and you are again imagining 1 minute movie & asking same interrogative questions. Now write down all the analysis about this relation from 2nd position. Dissociate from situation. Look around & sit at other chair.

- Imagine you are an independent neutral observer at 3rd position, and now replay the movie of two people at position 1 and 2, also ask the same interrogative questions. Now, if you want to improve this relationship what advice will you give to the person at perceptual position 1 (which is you only), which will cure the relation? You are also consulting with great people who are impartial to give needed advices & suggestions to person at position 1 which is yourself. Find minimum 2 advices and note down them.

- Now sit at position 4 which is super observer which is at even higher level and you can observe people at position 1, position 2 & position 3. Visualize same movie & ask same questions & recheck advices given by position no 3 if they are partial or good enough to improve this relationship. Old advices may be same or you may change it. You may give new advices if they can find out new solution in that relationship and note it down,

- Dissociate & again come at position 1, check notes and consider advices you have got from observers at positions 3 & 4. Start visualizing that you are following those advices. Now sit in chair of position 2 with whom you want to explore relationship. How the feelings of other person changing for this relationship after you have started following advices? This person will be partially ok now or he/she might be completely ok towards the relationship. Your neurons are getting programmed now for relationship betterment from your end. Now you will transfer your energy in this relation in a new way to relate with that person.

## PERSONAL EXPERIENCE ON EMPATHETIC THINKING

As we always say, every coin has 2 sides, if I talk about my childhood, cribbing or complaining about childhood will never give me solution or peace of mind. Yes, I can look at it from a new perspective - as I experienced such variations in my childhood that I have learnt to empathize with people around me. If I would not have gone through that phase, probably I would not have empathized with people so well. My empathetic thinking has come with my learning & experiences.

As roses come with thorns, beautiful relationships also come with small conflicts and arguments. When I and my beloved husband used to have fights, first I used to get disturbed for couple of days after arguments. But when I actually learnt and started applying emotional intelligence, I started explaining my anger instead of expressing it which resulted into solutions. I started effectively relaxing by using perceptual positions techniques and empathetically started thinking from his perspective and my anger also used to get lowered and my rational thinking started replacing my emotional thinking. I also associated negative aspects to my anger that if I am getting angry or emotionally unstable then it is increasing my cortisol level, I started creating inner voices that it's affecting me and my beauty which will result in hair fall, ageing or other issues hence it's high time that I should learn to relax my mind in such situations.

By using perceptual positions techniques with my husband, mother, brother and in-laws, life became smoother like never before. All things were sorted easily in my personal as well as professional life. It also resulted in my enhanced interpersonal and communication skills. There was absolutely no ambiguity.

The highest degree of empathy which I feel has developed between us- I & Vaibhav. How we work together is a perfect example of empathy. I know one thing very well when people come & build their business, I have always seen them **end  up in fighting** or **discussing majorly about money,** but truly speaking we are growing in our profession is just because of one thing ,we empathize with each other really very well & money is absolutely secondary in our lives. If today some contingency happens, I am so sure that both or one among us will always back out leaving everything for the other. Such a kind of great empathy we have developed & it has added lot of advantage in our business too. He understands that I have my family & responsibilities so he gives me space & handles my work accordingly, at the same time similarly I empathize with him for his working hours and workload of business. So I never end up losing my cool when sometimes professional things get procrastinated. My empathetic thinking results into rational and solution oriented approach which resolves the issue quickly.- **Shruti Chitlangia Dhruve**

## TIP FOR EMPATHETIC THINKING

Never rush to show empathy in haste and do not try to empathize with other person just for the sake of it or out of sympathy! We must truly understand other people's situation before empathizing with them. There is difference between empathy & sympathy. Empathy is when we put ourselves into shoes of other and think from their perspective whereas sympathy is feelings of sorrow for others misfortune. We should never make assumptions as assumptions are the enemy of empathy as they harbor preconceived biased notions that are not based on true understanding or experiences of others. We should always take extra time to listen and ask questions before trying to connect with the other person and solving the problem in relationship. The other person should never think about us that we don't listen to them & should withdraw them away from healthy communication with us. Always remember good communication & rapport is essential for empathetic thinking.

Empathy for each other is the secret behind our ever growing professional excellence!

> "Empathy is the unidirectional fast highway to travel the journey from anger to serenity"
> –Vaibhav Vasant Patil

## *CHAPTER 2.3*

## *BUILDING RAPPORT WITH PEOPLE*

Why does it happen with most of us that while we were in school & college, surrounded with many individuals, friends, colleagues, we had a strong rapport only with few selected people? Even in our professional life, we experience this. There are only few gifted people who are blessed to have excellent rapport with most of the people they meet due to their unique personality traits such as good interpersonal skills. If you want to prosper in your professional as well as personal life, then you must learn to build rapport with known or even unknown people. In the previous chapter, we learnt about empathetic thinking but for that, building rapport with the person with whom you need to empathize is important.

**WHAT IS RAPPORT?**

Rapport is a positive, close & harmonious relationship between individuals with mutual bonding, connect, trust, influence, respect, understanding and empathy. Often like-minded people have better rapport between them. Rapport enables more open minded communication. We meet many people every day, but only with some of them we can naturally build rapport, because there are certain factors of psychology associated with it and we need to work upon developing rapport building skills. One individual doesn't have rapport with other individuals until they have a good relationship with each other. **Rapport is not deliberate manipulation.** Empathy and ability to understand people's perspective is important for rapport building. Rapport building is the innate or developed ability to explore common things that both individuals can agree with. It includes body language & gestures which indicate connect, trust & understanding. Friendship or agreement with someone is not rapport. It is not necessary that if we agree with some people, it means we have good rapport with them; on the other hand we can have good rapport with some people even if we disagree with them. Sometimes we don't find good rapport with our family members, friends or relatives, but on the other hand we find excellent bonding and rapport even with a complete stranger.

## WHY IS IT IMPORTANT TO CREATE RAPPORT?

Rapport is a very important & essential element in personal and professional excellence for any individual. In personal aspects, relationship blossoms well when there is good rapport in terms of communication, empathy & mutual trust. Wellness in our personal relations is reflected in wellness in our professional life & vice versa. If we have good rapport with our family members and relatives, then there are very less chances of misunderstanding & distortion of facts. Due to enhanced rapport, we become more open to accept our mistakes or become more forgiving, satisfying and loyal. Playful relationships are built with rapport and not with just mere agreement.

(Images sources: First Image by <u>Gerd Altmannv</u> from <u>Pixabay</u> & Second image by rawpixel.com from Pixels)

**You can connect & create rapport with people only when you stop becoming judgmental about people & treat every person equally. Preconceived notion is a big barrier in creating rapport with people. When you come to the level in the context of communication, body postures & gestures, language etc. which constitute comfort level to the other person, then you will easily establish rapport with that person within no time.**

In professional aspects, rapport is one of the important criteria that the organizations and HR people see while hiring the candidates. Candidates, who have good technical skills and knowledge, often fail in interview because they fail to build rapport with interviewers. When we have been given a task in office, while executing it, we need to build rapport with our colleagues, seniors, juniors, team members to successfully accomplish the given task in the stipulated time. The absence of a good rapport often ends up in arguments, groupism and blame games, dirty politics etc. in professional life. In any business, rapport with clients and customers is the most important factor behind customer acquisition, retention & customer loyalty. A good rapport with customers also helps in a good word of mouth. Lack of good rapport can impact and influence the outcome of any conversation.

**HOW TO BUILD RAPPORT WITH PEOPLE?**

**Empathetic thinking & communication** are important aspects in order to build good rapport with any individual. Good rapport gets established when we learn to think from other's point of view. Taking time out and showing genuine interest for others with whom we want to establish rapport is important. We need to constantly pay attention to how they are thinking and what is going on in their mind. We need to enter into other persons' world as per their point of view by putting ourselves in their shoes and walking the road of life along with them which is often called as **'Pacing'**. This is generally followed by **'Leading'** when we capitalize on the rapport created and influence other person. Matching and mirroring with physiology i.e. body motions, posture, voice, speed, facial expressions, hand and leg movements, gestures of other person helps to build rapport and pace with other person. We can use **'Humor'to** build instant rapport with anyone or finding common areas of interest and references is also a good practice in building rapport. We should use people's name while addressing them which helps in long term rapport building. Once we learn the art of rapport building (more effectively with NLP & Emotional intelligence) then we can experience harmony and continuous improvement in our personal and professional life.

**RAPPORT BUILDING TECHNIQUE**

You can practice following rapport building technique with any unknown person or known persons from your personal or professional life.

- Meet the person at a good meeting place, coffee shop, home etc. depending on the relationship you hold with that person.
- Speak in the same Language as that of person. If 100% speaking in the language of that person is not possible, then try maximum to talk in the person's language (even if it's imperfect) in combination with other language which you know.
- Identify what type of person he/she is - is he/she visual, auditory or kinesthetic person? (Visual person gets clear idea about things visually.

Auditory person gets clear idea about things with audios and kinesthetic person likes to feel.)These types are also called as **representation types.**

- Once you get a judgment of person's **representation type** (refer types of people & their memory in memory techniques section), use language accordingly. For example, for visual person you may say that, **'I can see your pain.'**

- Match their speed of talking. Are they talking fast or slow?

- Match the tone & voice of the person. Are they talking loudly or in soft tone? Is tone rough or smooth?

- Now, match the breathing pattern of the person for which you need to have minute observation of his/her voice and nasal sounds & breathing patterns which involves breathing speed, frequency etc.

- After that, match the body posture of the person which includes spinal alignment, shoulder positions, chin position etc.

- Now observe their style, is it simple, dynamic, dashing, full of attitude or grounded?

- Mirror and match the exact style but take care that you are not making person in front of you conscious. The person should not think that you are imitating or mimicking him/ her.

- Try to connect emotionally with the person for which first you need to get aware of his/ her emotions.

- Do identify some common interests with that person and reinforce those common interests in communication. E.g. sports, cooking, dancing etc.
- The more and more factors you will match and mirror of the person in front, the better will be rapport.

## PERSONAL EXPERIENCE ON RAPPORT BUILDING

Since childhood I was a single girl brought up in joint family. I never got enough love and attention of my parents as they stayed away from me due to work and also they never compromised with my studies, so they kept me at my native place with my relatives. Since childhood, I started getting empathized with people. Even before becoming an Emotional Intelligence Expert, I could easily get empathized with students and their issues and helped them solving it due to my empathetic nature. Apart from training profession, I am also a senior lecturer in many institutes of CA, ACCA, and CS etc. I remember there was one student who used to be quiet during lectures. He seemed depressed. One day after lecture, I met him and tried to make him speak his mind out, only when I came to know that he had attempted suicide twice. I made my rapport stronger with him by matching and mirroring his personality traits such as voice, body language, etc. I thought empathetically from his perspective and things became clearer as why and how he was suffering. With this rapport, I asked him to do some NLP & EI activities.

He was very comfortable after that day. Gradually he started smiling; he was in a better state of mind, speaking with other students playfully and with an open mind. He was no more in depressed state. I built rapport with him; in return, he did same with other students and opened up his mind in a good way. In my professional life too, with our clients in public & corporate training programs, we use rapport techniques to build a bond and make them feel comfortable so people speak out their problems, don't hesitate to disclose details which makes us give them exact solution and therapy.

There have been many instances in my teaching profession, wherein my students get motivated from me, feels connected with me and appreciates me due to my good rapport building skill. One student always keeps me telling, "Madam, you are still underutilizing yourself. You are capable of doing everything on the earth. You are a good orator, a good professor, a good human being, a good mother and as far as I know you are a great house maker. You can go in any industry be it beauty contest and you will definitely emerge as a winner. You have such a unique personality." I had taught him few years back when he was my student; he couldn't converse in English properly and wanted to improve his communication skills. He wanted to be confident and see a change in his life. There were certain guidelines which I gave to him and today wherever he goes he cracks every interview. He talks with everyone confidently and makes sure to leave an impact and spark everywhere he goes. He has changed his personality, but still a long way to reach for him as the saying goes 'sky is the limit' and 'learning is a never ending process'.

I would also like to share another sweet experience of what could be a better trophy than this if you can build good rapport with others. It is a feeling of bliss for me. I met my student on a social networking platform after few years. As I was not much active on social site, he couldn't get to connect with me. He was very happy to get in touch with me again and praised me a lot. He stated that I was his idol from the start. It gave me a good feeling from within and suddenly one best thing came out which gave me a pleasant surprise. He said, "Madam, I am married, my baby girl is three months old and I have kept her name 'Shruti' that much I respect, adore and idolize you. Thank you for changing my life completely." Friends, a good rapport is like a seed of happiness which if you sow at the right time in the right way, you will get lifelong bliss in terms of love, care and respect from people in your personal and professional life.

**– Shruti Chitlangiya Dhruve.**

## TIP FOR RAPPORT BUILDING

### How to Build a Rapport on Telephone Voice Call?

On telephone voice call, we can't match the physiology of the person on the other side unless it is a video call. In such case, matching voice, tonality, volume, speed and pauses of that person on call works in building rapport with that person. Always open a call with a smile as it relaxes and welcomes other person on a good note. Often use the name of the person on call to get connected with that person. Right humor at right time plays vital role in creating instant rapport with person on call or face to face. Ask some **'Ice breaking questions'** to other person such as 'How is your day?', 'How are you?' etc.

This ensures we are human and not robots meant to follow only work instructions, then take the call ahead. Be a good listener which will indicate that you are mentally engaged in the process and ensure good mutual understanding. Acknowledge in such a way to let the person on other side understand that you are listening for which you can use **'responders'** such as 'okay', 'yes', 'sounds good', etc. Use the similar language and words the other person uses on call. Use words which will indicate empathetic connect with other person such as 'I can understand your point of view', 'I agree with you', 'you are right at your place', and 'I would have done the same if I would have been at your place' etc.

Good rapport during lectures or workshop always makes our students &participants to surround & have an interaction with us!

More than elegant & intellectual personality, it's due to our rapport, that every batch of students or participants always take selfies with us.

*"Rapport is the win-win tool for achieving your desired outcomes with the help of people"*
*-Shruti Chitlangiya Dhruve*

## CHAPTER 2.4

## CHANGING STATE OF MIND

Are you a moody person? Does your mood change frequently? Do you feel depressed at some time and then feel ecstatic next hour? You might have faced such mood swings sometime in your life.

The problem there was external events or triggers that were controlling your moods or state of mind. In Emotional Intelligence, as per Goldman's model we deal with becoming aware of our own emotions, because only after that we can manage them and changing state is a handy tool to change & manage our emotions in resourceful manner. You might be aware that many old people advise us to go at some other place for picnic or trip if we are not feeling good mentally or health wise, it's only because change of place changes our state of mind and we come in a resourceful state to manage our emotions in a better way.

What you used to do during exams as you had to study for many long hours and you used to get bore by sitting at one place or studying same subject? You might have preferred to go for a walk, watch TV, and listen to music or even changing studies to your favorite subject to change your state of mind to resourceful state. Remaining in resourceful state is important to excel in life. **People don't lack resources but they lack resourceful state.**

## WHAT IS STATE?

**It is sum total of neurophysiologic process of thoughts, emotions & physical energy at a given point of time.** It is the way of being in any moment. We can say the state is a mood at the specific time. The state is a psychological state of someone's cognitive processes & personal internal representation at a specific time which is the current condition or character of a person's thoughts or feelings.

**States are of two types:**

- **Constructive or Resourceful state:** In this state we use our available resources for producing optimal results. It includes Confidence, Happiness, Delightfulness, Concentration, Ecstasy, Decision making, Love, Flexibility, Playfulness etc.
- **Destructive or Unresourceful state:** In this state we become literally inefficient & unproductive even if we have some resources. It includes fear, phobia, trauma, sadness, guilt, discomfort, confusion, depression, frustration etc.

**We get into resourceful state when there is healthy balance between emotions & mind. We take rational, productive decisions in resourceful state of mind.**

The State is created by our five senses. We perceive any event through five senses i.e. visual, auditory, touch, smell & taste.

## WHY IS IT IMPORTANT TO CHANGE STATE?

It is important to change our state from destructive to constructive as we can't waste our time & resources by being into a destructive state of mind. We are completely dissociated from our present when we are in unresourceful state because we are thinking about something else rather than being in our present work which is very inefficient condition. Another problem is that in an unresourceful state we experience distance from our bodily sensations which may lead to numbness. Our body secretes negative hormones such as cortisol, adrenaline & stress hormones which causes many health issues. Hence for physical, mental, personal & professional wellbeing it is essential to change the unresourceful state into a resourceful state.

## HOW TO CHANGE STATE?

Changing state is a process, where we break ourselves from our routine & therefore change our emotional state from what we were going through. This is called **Emotional Shift** or **Change of State**. We can change state by changing our physiology i.e. our posture, facial expressions, breathing patterns & inner voices. Our emotions & mental state are associated with our physiology as we know when we get angry or excited, our breathing pattern, facial expressions changes.

(Background image source: By Mikegi from Pixabay)

**HUMAN VIBRATIONS**

| RAISING | LOWERING |
|---|---|
| GRATITUDE | TOXIC RELATIONSHIP |
| KINDNESS | NEGATIVE THOUGHTS |
| LOVE | ARGUING |
| JOY | RADIATIONS |
| PASSION | YELLING |
| FORGIVENESS | HOLDING ONTO PAST |
| ACCEPTANCE | ANGER |
| SUNSHINE | RESENTMENT |
| WALKING IN NATURE | GUILT |
| BREATHING DEEPLY | MEDICATION |
| YOGA,EXERCIZE | WHITE SUGAR |
| LAUGHING,SMILING | TOXIC PRODUCTS |
| HUGGING | EXCESS RED MEAT |
| SINGING | ENVIRONMENTAL TOXIC |
| DANCING | HARD ALCHOHOL |
| RAW WHOLE FOODS | JUNK FOOD |
| GREENS,FRUITS,NUTS | |
| RELAXING MUSIC | |
| CREATIVITY | |

**We should always change our state from lowering to raising vibrations to attract positive things with similar vibrations from the universe.**

Hence in changing physiology, we do the reverse i.e. we control our emotions & state of mind by changing our physiology. We can also change our state by changing internal representations. We can change state with our five senses by listening to music, jogging Up & Down the stairs, visualizing or recollecting happy incidences, meditation, dance, physical exercise, drinking water, sleeping, body massage, bath etc. We should never stick to our unresourceful state for long, as it goes on escalating. Once we get conviction that we are solely in control of our emotions, we can move away from bad moods and learn to exist in a beautiful state, any time.

**"SUPPOSE I AM" TECHNIQUE:**

We can change our state by changing events which we have perceived in our mind. We can also change state by moving our body differently as mind and body is one and interconnected.

This technique can be used for creating states of happiness, confidence, worthiness, being loved etc. When you get depressed - your shoulders drop, when you get angry-your face becomes red. Whenever you get fear-there are movements in your gut. Now we will control body to control mind. By 'Suppose I am' technique. Whatever state you want to gain you can get it. For happiness you will just say, 'Suppose I am a happy person'. It is an instant state maker. There will be four things in it to control.

**1. Body**

**2. Breathing**

**3. Facial expressions**

**4. Internal voice.**

If we program those 4 things, then our body will control our mind. If you say yourself 'suppose I know..."Suppose I am __' then your mind and body get impacted. When people will get depressed, they will have shallow breathing. Their facial expressions will get affected. Let's try this technique for 'Confidence'. Say yourself that , 'I am (your name) and suppose I am becoming confident.' .If you are using 'becoming' instead of 'I am ' then your mind also supports commands realistically.

- Put your spine in confident body language by saying yourself that, 'suppose I am confident'. Now put your shoulder position as if you are really confident.
- Breathe in a way that, as if you are confident. Keep breathing that way. Create such wonderful breathing for next 1 minute.
- Bring your facial expressions as if you are fully confident.
- Create internal voices such as 'hey, I am confident', 'I am smart'. Bring this state full of confidence at peak. Listen voices from every organ, every cell of your body that you are confident.
- Supposing you are confident put your chin as if you are looking towards sky.
- Keep repeating in your mind that - I am becoming confident. Open your eyes. Do one more time. Understand. Result will come in 2-3 minutes. This technique can do magic. If someone tells you that

'he or she doesn't know how to do something', then you can say – Suppose you know you can do it. If a person comes to you, ask him suppose he is feeling good with all four aspects? Physical state is important. This technique works even better if you can create an anchor with it.

- Go into the time when you used to feel confident. You used to win prizes, when you have got good marks, others used to appreciate you, and how you used to smile! Make those pictures bigger, brighter, and closer. As if you are enjoying, put your shoulders, have long breaths, facial expressions. Create internal voices, as 'hey I am feeling confident.' Create wonderful voices. Go in that time & from that past a beautiful energy has started coming towards you. Put some colors in that energy storm. Energy is coming towards you in the form of a fresh breath of air & encircling around you. You are inhaling this wonderful energy throughout your body. You are enjoying feeling of confidence. You are having wonderful pictures on mental screen. Picture should be 3d, colorful, brighter. Create an anchor with it and reuse it whenever you want feeling of confidence.

## PERSONAL EXPERIENCE ON CHANGING STATE OF MIND (state change):

There are multiple examples I can give on state change, but I strongly relate this along with trivial fights which keeps happening with every person and in every family. Whenever I got in an argument with anyone in my family or friends, I used to get disturbed and sometimes end up stretching it for many days. Now, after my learning's on NLP & EI, things got clear to me that if I think much about the incident and don't change my state of mind at the right time, then it will surely waste my present and my current moment. In fact, not just the current moment but even my future because of my bitter past which has happened and will never be changed. So, after any conflicts, I started pause therapy and then focused on changing my mindset from negative to neutral or positive state. Now I don't get myself affected and refrain stretching anything for the next days as I quickly change my state and try to be happy by engaging and focusing myself on the available resources in my hand such as going for a drive, doing workout, sipping a coffee in a coffee shop or playing with my son.

It is not a big thing if I say I always had a good work life balance. There are lots of people who know well and also provide trainings on how to balance professional and personal life. In context with changing mindset, I will say when you are balancing; you are either compromising or affecting certain hormones in your body. I am not talking about compromising in anything. It is all about changing the state of mind according to the situation and the person concerned. Lacking in this means you are hurting yourself or the person who is expecting something from you. Let me give you a personal example. As a mother, sometimes it becomes very difficult for me to balance personal and professional things. I have hectic schedules, and take 12 hours lectures a day when required. There are clients to whom I attend personally and heal them. You can understand I go through lot of variations and traumatic conditions of people around me. Before I heal them, I first empathize and understand them where it hits me from within and my inner voice keeps making me feel exhausted and tired after long working hours. But when I go back home, I know only one thing that the moment I step inside my house, I belong to my family and my son. Then immediately I have to change the state of my mind which I know I could do only because of this learning of implementing the mind state change.

**- Shruti Chitlangiya Dhruve**

**TIP TO CHANGE STATE:**

**PLANING YOUR MOODS!**

A busy person who wants to reach his goal will always plan, so every morning plans your moods. The way you plan your activities, plan your moods & program it in the morning & check your responses, feelings, state for 1 minute every hour. Are you powerful, peaceful or energetic? **Then accept the things.** Don't change your situations, change your thoughts & be stable. For example, at 7am when you wake up in morning, you can plan your mood as, blissful to start the day, at 9am as energetic before you commence your work, 2 am joyful, 6pm relaxed after completing your work & at 12am in midnight as optimistic before you close eyes & sleep.

# PLAN YOUR MOODS

| TIME | MOODS |
|------|-------|
| 06:00 AM | CALM |
| 8:00 | BLISSFUL |
| 10:00 | ENERGETIC |
| 12:00 | CONTENT |
| 02:00 | JOYFUL |
| 04:00 | LAZY |
| 06:00 | RELAXED |
| 08:00 | HAPPY |
| 10:00 | LOVING |
| 12:00 | OPTIMISTIC |

**Plan your moods & learn to control your emotions.**

In between our workshop session, we ask students & participants to share jokes to change state.

Going through good & happy visual memories can be an effective state change activity!

> *"Never take any permanent decision due to your temporary state of mind, which is changeable within a few minutes"-Vaibhav Vasant Patil*

# *CHAPTER 2.5*

# *LIVING IN PRESENT*

Have you ever organized any small or big event? If you have, then you must have realized that you don't enjoy that event to the fullest as other people who are participants or audiences enjoy. If our example is making sense to you, can you think of why this happens? On a more serious note, people are able to live their daily routine life with open, issueless mind & there is lack of fully fledged happiness in their daily life! Has it ever happened with you that your next paper or entire exam is spoilt just because you messed up in your first paper and you were unable to focus on your upcoming papers in exam due to fear of the result of first paper? The reason behind this is we think about past mistakes and worry too much about future. 'Enjoy each & every moment of life!', a very famous quote we often notice during seminars, messages, on social networking sites, television, in various motivational seminars ,on YouTube sessions & even we hear it from our friends, relatives & family etc. Can you think and tell me, how a conservancy worker (drainage cleaner) or railway tracks laborer working 12 -

15 hours a day with one or zero holidays per week can enjoy each and every moment of his life? We have just learned how to think empathetically, right? Now can you empathize with this conservancy worker? He cannot even avoid his work due to supervisors on field! No chance for him to use mobiles for chatting or interacting with his wife or family! Even he will go home; he will end up sleeping as he is tired! What type of life are people living? We are not commenting on their standards of living or lack of abilities but we are talking about how they will get happiness in their daily routines? In fact, the people who say that,' we should enjoy each and every moment of life', what kind of enjoyment even they are living in their routine? One day picnics, one day lunch or dinner, party, birthday celebrations & such stuff cannot be called as living each and every ,moment or living in present if you are in a dissociated state from whatever you are doing.

**WHAT IS LIVING IN PRESENT?**

Living in present means being in "Right Here, Right Now". Living in present means using all our five senses & internal awareness completely for present moment. In this all our attention & conscious mind is completely focused in the things which we are doing in present. We don't think & get affected with negative feelings from past and we also don't worry about future, because when we focus in present, it automatically directs our attention away from past & ensures better future. When we are completely in present, we are not deviated & distracted from current moment which may be the task at hand, talking with person, driving, going out for dinner with family etc. We are fully conscious & self-awareness is at its peak at any moment when we are in present. Our thought process proceeds with time when we live in present, it means, when we get up in morning at 7am,we will think only about morning ambience, resetting our bed & other things and we will think 'What is next now?' & we will proceed for those morning activities such as brushing teeth, having breakfast, talking with our family etc. In real life, contrary to this living in present, we end up rushing in morning hours; we get tense about how we will spend our day! How we will accomplish our targets in office! How we will manage client in meeting! What if I get late! Such kind of thinking spoils our entire day, our worries gets converted into reality! Practically thinking, as we are human beings with unstable ,unpredictable minds, it's not always possible to live in present as our mind keeps thinking about problems, events, future events at conscious & subconscious level which results in inventions, ideas, solutions, planning & many other good things also; still we should learn & ensure we are living in the present at vital & critical moments of our life such as doing worship, celebrating birthdays of self and others, writing the examination, talking with spouse etc.

**WHY IS IT IMPORTANT TO LIVE IN THE PRESENT?**

The pages of life get unfolded with present but most of the time we let this present go without utilizing it at its best. We are always busy in doing something, especially after evolution of digital and internet era. Remember! Living in virtual present and in real present -there is a huge difference. We lose calmness, mindfulness and 'Me Time' we don't give much time to get awareness of our thoughts and emotions. When we are in school or college, most of us have experienced that we fantasies about getting holidays and when we finally get holidays, instead of enjoying full in holidays we worry about results and also eagerly wait for school or college to start.

Most of the time, it happens that we dwell in our past or worry about our future and don't focus in the present moment. This lack of absence in present helps us neither to rectify nor change our past. On the other hand, it ends up spoiling our future. We spend lot of our time in other moments or futile work than focus on the present moment or work in hand such as we operate our mobiles when we are in important lecture or workshop, we focus our attention on TV, while having lunch or dinner at home; we tend to surf internet when we are making some document on our laptop, our life is full of distractions, which is affecting our present & we are subjected to unhealthy patterns. Our hasty & chaotic life doesn't help us to be in present.

Living in present ensures our life is smooth, sorted & undistracted. Our relationships, business, career can revive at its best if we learn to live in present in these important domains. Living in present brings us in a resourceful state where we manage our distractions & get focused on the current moment where we experience being in full flow & highest level of efficiency &productivity in professional life & better empathy &

connect with our loved ones in our personal life. Considering our fast lifestyles & our tendency to dwell in past & worry about future, we get anxiety, stress and unhappiness which we may not even realize, but this can cause our body to secrete  bad hormones such as cortisol which may affect us mentally& physically and leaves us pessimistic and frustrated .

TV or newspaper advertisements, reminders, texts, notifications, or online messages and alerts are all often inclined towards the past or the future which keep on disturbing us. The best solution for this is a conscious awareness and a commitment to living in the "now moment". It propels us to be more aware, happier, healthier, more focused, less stressed, less worried & more in control.

**HOW TO LIVE IN PRESENT?**

We can fantastically live in present by using all our five senses which are generally disintegrated. In this we need to consciously use each of our five senses while doing task in hand. For example, suppose you are doing workout in gym, then how can we live in present moment by applying our five senses? First of all five senses are auditory, visual, kinesthetic (touch), smell & taste. In gym, while doing workout we can use visual sense as observing others and gym trainers doing workout where we observe their form & techniques. We can also internally visualize us doing our workout in a best way. We hear countdowns, pain voices by people doing workouts. We can also create internal motivating voices such, 'I can do it', and 'I am able'. We can use our kinesthetic sense by sensing our bodily & muscle movements, body temperature, perspiration etc. To get away with stench of perspiration we can apply perfume smell it where we use our sense of smell.

(Image source: First image by MiguelA.Padrinan from Pexels&

Second image by George Becker from Pexels)

**Solving puzzles, su-do-ku, doing calculations mentally trying to by heart the things are one of the best ways to live in present moment. You will do everything unsuccessfully till you get fully in present!**

We can have some energy drinks; pre or post workout drinks etc. and use our taste sense. While doing all these things consciously, we realize that we are completely living in present moment & doing our workout at highest level of efficiency & capacity. To do good in present, we can also think about our past or future in a positive way. We can look at our past mistakes or instances, find positive intentions behind them & learn from them.

Instead of worrying about future, we can plan our future well in advance & this way we can balance our past & future to make our present better. Apart from that, there are many other techniques to live in the present moment such as body scanning, writing diary or pages, yoga, mind yoga, bringing more acceptance, focusing on breath & doing breathing techniques, associating pleasure to be in present & associating pain for dwelling into past or future.

**'RIGHT HERE RIGHT NOW' TECHNIQUE**

- Find a secluded natural place like garden, riverside, jungle like places etc.
- Close your eyes. Apply your five senses. See and try to get judgments of the pictures on your mental screen. If there are pictures, make them blur and let them diminish in darkness. If you are hearing some internal sounds such as, 'How I will pay my EMI's?' 'I cannot pass this exam' etc. Then touch your forefinger and thumb of right hand and mute all these sounds.
- Now count even numbers in a reverse way such as 100, 98, 96 ....till 2.This will counter the you're though process about other things.
- Now just try consciously to listen to external sounds of birds, animals, flowing water etc. Focus your entire attention on external sounds. Try to perceive those sounds as music
- Now let's use our kinesthetic sense. Feel the temperature of air around you. Feel the touch of wind around you.

- Now open your eyes. Start observing each natural element. Touch the flower or leaves of tree. Feel their texture. Try to find more than one color in them. See its shine. Touch the water, take it in your hands and release it as if you are releasing your past traumas. Touch the ground, take some earth in your hands and release it as if you are releasing your worries of future.

- Now, take any flower in your hand. Smell it and let that smell flow throughout your body. You are only applying your olfactory sense now. Similarly smell the earth, water, leaves and put in mind in such a s way that you will always memorize it

- Now, pluck any fruit, flower or leaf. Take it closer to your nose, smell it. Also feel its texture. Now, take a small bite of it. Chew it and try to use your gustatory sense of taste. What kind of taste it is? After that drink water from river before smelling it & feeling its viscosity.

- Now sit again at your place. You will realize that you are free from any thoughts of past or future start doing everything with conscious awareness now. You will realize that you are in full focus of self.

- Friends, congrats you're conscious, subconscious mind and five senses for giving such amazing experience of living in presence.

**PERSONAL EXPERIENCE FOR LIVING IN PRESNCE:**

I remember days of my best friend post her delivery phase when her baby used to be very small. After her pregnancy phase, she started working. She had kept a house maid specially to attend her baby as well as for household works, but the problem with her maid was she used to remain absent without proper intimation and also she used to intimate about her 3 to 4 days holidays all of a sudden. My friend was dependent on her so she used to panic and end up affecting entire day. Not only this , but when her maid used to inform her about her sudden holidays , she used to end up taking tension from the very day when her maid used to inform and her next three to four days (even before maid remain absent) used to get ruined .Now the question was what was to be done?

I had also faced similar situation as I had also kept a maid with consent of my family members to look after my baby and other household works, as I have to be out of home for my long lectures or training programs, but when similar situations of non availability of my maid used to happen, I never let it affect me or my family. I remember I guided my friend with my own example. My question for myself or her used to be  that, 'maid will be leaving after 2 days then why we are spoiling our 2 days from now?'

Let those 2 days pass, enjoy those 2 days, whatever is going to be happen will  as it is going to be happen. If you think about it now, you will spoil your two days including the days when she is not going to come. I believe , 'live in present, think well, plan it well, your days will come, enjoy those two days and may be with a nice, clear head planning you will be able to cope up with those days when she will not be there. As it is she not going to be there, nothing is going to change, the only change you need to undergo is in your thinking. My readings and life experiences say that, 'if you believe, if you create surroundings, if you use your five senses for low of attraction, you will get support from the universe to give you those vibrations back that is why we say if you know and you believe things are in your hands, the universe is definitely going to bless you with it and that is what happened with me. My positive thinking & positive vibrations attracted positive support from my, family members who took care of my households and my baby whenever possible, when my maid was not available and I had professional commitments.

With my friend, I realized that all this was affecting her due to her own thoughts and state of mind and not actually due to maid. I asked her to start accepting that she is not going to come that day or for the next couple of days or week. I asked her to start focusing on tasks at hand at the present moment. For better focus, I asked her to apply all five senses. In my case, I used to start finding some rational and logical solutions of managing my house works and my baby's day, where my family members helped me. Even after that if any problem arose, and then I used to take action in search of rational solutions rather cribbing on the consequences. The same I conveyed to my friend and now she tackles the problem in a better way

**- Shruti Chitlangia Dhruve**

**TIP TO LIVE IN PRESENCE:**

One good way to learn to be more in present is by slowly eliminating mindless activities from our routine. For example watching movies or reality shows on TV whenever we are at home, takes us away from our own present life & we end up entering & getting attached with present life of celebrities & actors on TV. So, if we want to increase our mindfulness for better present, then it is best if we can limit or eliminate mindless activities such as watching TV, using mobile phones for virtual games, surfing unproductive things on internet, using social networking site for 24 hours etc.(these activities might change your state for temporary time but not recommendable for living in present)& replacing those mindless activities with mindful activities with all five senses involved in it such as doing exercise, going on walk with family or friends, playing physical games, solving puzzles, going out for coffee, lunch or dinner, reading books, playing outdoor games, engaging healthy talks & discussions with people etc.

Practically speaking we can't always live in present moment as you know we get almost 80,000 thoughts in a day,but we can live in present moment when that moment or people in those moments are important.Changing state before living in present moment helps a lot.

'Living in presence' activity during 'outbound' training conducted by Shareskills Trainers.

Women cricket team after winning the tournament conducted by Shareskills. We not only conduct sports, games, physical activities but we also give rewards & recognition to winners.

*"Absence from 'past' & present in 'now' balance our future anyhow!"-Vaibhav Vasant Patil*

# PART 3

# HOW TO GET BLISS

# WITH

# HUMAN MEMORY TECHNIQUES

# CHAPTER 3.1

# INTRODUCTION TO HUMAN MEMORY

Is Human Memory power important in today's digital world of computers, smart phones, tablets & artificial intelligence? Today's world is a digital world. Many people might think that due to digitization, the dependency of people on human memory power has decreased due to innovative devices & artificial intelligence. But the fact is that nothing can replace the importance of human memory power as even to access mobiles or laptops people need basic human memory. Presently, from KG to PG, human memory power plays important role. In our daily life, our memory is essential in case of bank transactions, scheduling our busy routines & business or job-related aspects. We get hurt or panicky if we forget our valuables or when we don't get the right things at right time. Our memory helps make us who we are today.

Human memory is essential in today's fast & quick world & it cannot be replaced by artificial intelligence. Students, employees or businessmen who are good in memorizing are perceived to be intelligent, smart & are given priority in their respective fields or domains. People with good memory get appreciation & recognition in their professional as well as personal life!   Hence if you want to excel in your life & with full confidence, then getting aware of your memory & learning to apply it is important.

## HOW EXACTLY HUMAN MEMORY WORKS?

More than numbers, letters, words & theories, there are lots of other things which our brain memorizes. E.g. baby's first talk, the taste of your mother's delicious food, the smell of perfume of any special person. These are memories that make up ongoing experience of our life; they provide us with a sense of self. They tie our past with our present, and provide a framework for the future.

Do you remember what you had in your last lunch? The image & sub modalities (size, color, shape, temperature etc.) of a plate of a meal with various foods come into your mind. Our "memory" is made up of a group of systems that each plays a different role in creating, storing, and recalling our memories.

It seems that there is a single memory but memorization is a collection of multiple memories. If you think of an object-a mobile, then your brain retrieves the object's brand name & its sub modalities -its shape, its function, the sound when it rings, its body texture etc. Yet you're never aware of these separate mental experiences, nor that are they coming from all different parts of your brain, as they all work together so well.

(Image Resource: Belle on buffer.com)

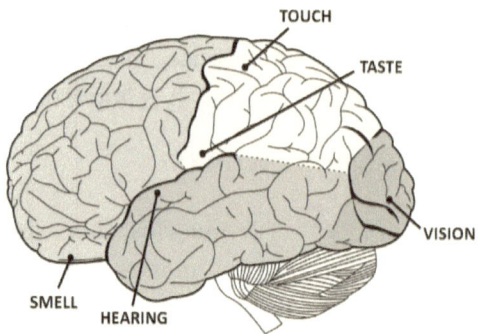

**Our brain memorizes things easily with the help of our five senses.**

**Encoding** is the first step in creation of memory. It's a biological factor, in the senses, that begins with our perception (perception can be taken a personal reception via our senses). Let's take an example-the memory of the first vehicle you ride. When you bought that vehicle, your visual system registers physical features such as the color of the vehicle and its design. Our auditory system may have picked up the knocking sound of their ignition. You might also remember the vehicle's body texture.

These different sensory signals travelled to the relevant part of your brain - **The Hippocampus**, which integrated these perceptions as single experience, i.e. your complete experience of that specific vehicle.

(Image Resource: Wikimedia commons)

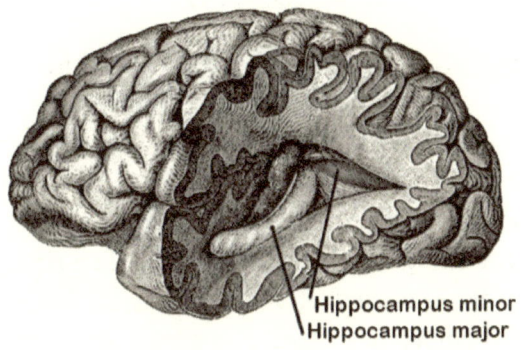

Hippocampus minor
Hippocampus major

**The Hippocampus** is a small, curved part in the brain which is responsible for the formation of new memories and is also associated with learning and emotions.

**Block Diagram For Brain Functioning**

As per experts, the hippocampus with **Frontal Cortex** which is the other part of brain analyzes these various sensory inputs and remembers them. If they are worth remembering & appealing to our five senses then they may become part of long-term memory.

Although a memory begins with reception of sensory inputs & perceptions, it is encoded and stored using the language of electricity and chemicals. Nerve cells connect with other cells at a point called a **'Synapse'** where all the action in your brain occurs & electrical pulses carrying messages jumps across gaps between cells.

If you play a piano for example, the repeated firing of certain cells in a certain order in your brain makes it easier to repeat this firing later on. The result is you get better at playing the piano. You can play it faster, with fewer mistakes. Consistent practice will make it perfect. Yet if you stop practicing for several weeks and then try to play piano, you may notice that the result is no longer perfect as your memory has started to forget what you once have learned and practiced perfectly because the neural associations with five senses were not strong enough to keep it for long term goals.

You must first pay attention to the thing which you want to memorize. Since you cannot pay selective attention to everything which comes across you all the time, most of what you come across every day is simply auto-deleted and only a few stimuli pass into your conscious awareness (Deletion in NLP language).

Our brain has around one billion neurons & each neuron forms about 1,000 connections to other neurons, to form more than a trillion connections. If each neuron could only store a single memory, then running out of space would become a problem. We have only a few gigabytes of storage space, which is similar to the memory space in electronic or data storage devices. Neurons combine to store many memories at a time, exponentially increasing the brain's memory storage capacity to around 2-3 petabytes (or a million gigabytes). So, if your brain would have remembered every single information at every moment, then your memory would be full in few minutes only. In applying memory techniques, how much of it you actually remember depends on how you pay attention to the desired information with your five senses accordingly to have stronger associations with hippocampus & parts of brain related to memory.

**TYPES OF PEOPLE & THEIR MEMORY:**

**VISUAL:** Visual people grasp better with visuals & motions, unlike sounds or kinesthesia. They like to see PowerPoint slides or videos which strike a chord with their memory.

**AUDITORY:** Auditory people grasp better with audios, sounds & rhymes rather than visuals. They like to listen lectures, audios etc.

**KINESTHETIC:** These people get information easily from touch, emotions & instincts. E.g. rather than seeing a cricket match on television or listening to commentary, they would rather play cricket & enjoy.

## WHAT ARE MEMORY PATTERNS? OR CUES OF HUMAN BRAIN?

Our brain has a specific pattern & cues to memorize the information.

- **INTEREST:**
  The things in which we are interested, we can memorize them easily.
  E.g. we can memorize data related with game in which we are interested.

- **ASSOCIATION:**
  The things with which we associate with, we tend to memorize them.
  E.g. If we associate our studies or profession with our better future, then we can do it, more efficiently.

- **COLOUR:**
  Our brain easily memorizes colors & imprints them easily in our memory.
  E.g. Colors are used in brand logos, book text highlighting & in cartoons to get associated with human brain easily.

- **MOTION:**
  Motion appeals to auditory memory & when we see motion, animations etc. our brain easily retains & recall things.

- **SIZE:**
  The brain retains & recalls things which are big in size. E.g. we tend to memorize big size food, people or cars.

- **SOUNDS:**
  Our brain memorizes the things which we relate with sounds.
  E.g. we can easily memorize a song if it has good sound and background music.

- **I, ME-MORE:**
  Our brain memorizes the things which are related with us. E.g. we never forget our own birthday but we tend to forget birthdates of others.

- **UNIQUE:**
  Unique things easily get imprinted into memories. E.g. we never forget a person with unique body features.

- **WEIRD:**
  Weirdness is the easy click for memory. E.g. If we see a human with two heads, we will memorize that event & relevant things such as that specific day, time, people around etc. for our lifetime.

- **FUNNY:**
  Funny memories & things are always preserved in our brains. E.g. If we try to memorize our school or college friends, then generally we tend to remember funny people. We still remember funny cartoons from our childhood.

- **RHYMES AND SONGS:**
  Poems, theories, passages, sentences etc. which are received in combination with **Rhymes & Songs** are always easy to memorize. E.g. Although the language of National anthem of India is difficult but only because of its passionate &

motivational rhymes, all educated people memorize it.

- **DISPROPORTIONATE:**
  Our brain easily catches disproportion. E.g. we easily memorize jokes of ants & elephants due to the basic disproportion between them.

- **EXTREME VARIATIONS/EMOTIONS:**
  We memorize the things, events & people with whom our extreme emotions are attached. E.g. we always memorize the things where our emotions have been involved such as fights, love, insults etc.

## MEMORY EXERCISES

Exactly as weight training in gym add muscles to our body & life years, similarly following a healthy lifestyle and performing regularly targeted brain exercises can also increase & reserve our brain's cognitive power .

### 1. Check Your Memory's Recall Power:

Make a list of anything such as your resolutions, mistakes, items to purchase from market, name of people etc. The longer the list, better it is. Then after every 2 hours, see how many items you recall. To get better impact, try to make items in list as challenging as possible.

**2. Do Basic Calculations Visually:** Try to do simple addition, multiplication & other mathematical operations without using pen & paper.

**3. Draw A Map:** Whenever you will visit new places, try to draw its map on paper, it will increase your recalling power.

## MEMORY TIPS

A) Always explore cooking new food items-As per NLP, stronger the five senses, stronger its relevant memory power. Cooking new things, strikes our five senses, hence it is good exercise to boost our memory.

B) Take out your old album & look at a photograph of your family. What memories does it bring back? Focus on one of the memories, trying to visualize it, recalls sounds, smells, and other sensations as well as what things you looked in that memory. Then write about it, recreating the scene & feel it.

## WHAT ARE THE FOOD ITEMS THAT CAN BE INCLUDED IN DIET TO IMPROVE MEMORY?

**1) Coffee:** Two main components in coffee — caffeine and antioxidants help your brain. It increases alertness, improves mood & sharpens concentration.

**2) Blueberries:** Animal studies have shown that blueberries help improve memory and may even delay short-term memory loss

**3) Turmeric:** Cur-cumin, the ingredient in turmeric, crosses the blood-brain barrier, meaning it can directly enter the brain and benefit the cells there. It erases depression & helps brain cells to grow.

**4) Almonds:** Almonds is considered "brain food." It contains healthy levels of vitamin E which prevent cognitive decline, boost alertness and preserve memory longer.

**5) Walnuts:** Walnut fight against memory loss. Even small consumption in a day improves cognitive function of brain.

**MEMORY TECHNIQUES:**

**1) PEGGING:**

Pegging system is like taking an object and hanging it on already prepared **'Peg'** in our memory. A peg system is a Memory technique for memorizing any lists using a Peg List which is predefined on the basis of Audio (rhymes), Visuals etc. It works by pre-memorized list of words that are easy to associate with the numbers they represent. Peg list is to be memorized only one time & then can be associated with many other objects. A peg word system is a predefined list that uses words as pegs. A Number

Rhyme System is one of the examples of a peg word system.

Each number from 1 to 10 can be given a rhyming mnemonic keyword: (A list on basis of Number Shapes can also be formed)

**One - gun**

**Two - shoe**

**Three - tree**

**Four - door**

**Five - knife**

**Six - Vicks**

**Seven - heaven**

**Eight - gate**

**Nine - wine**

**Ten - hen**

If you have a list of things to memorize, like a shopping list, you can associate each item of the list with a number rhyme image. So if your shopping list is: carrots, milk, bread, eggs etc. Then make associations like this: One is "gun" -- imagine a gun shooting a pile of carrots, the first item on your shopping list.

Two is "shoe" -- imagine cleaning your muddy shoe with a bottle of milk.

Three is "tree" -- imagine breads are hanging on a tree.

Four is "door" -- imagine throwing eggs at a door.

Once you've associated each item in your shopping list with a number peg, you'll be able to mentally walk through the numbers, recall the rhymes ("what was the gun shooting?") and recall the item ("carrots").You can also memorize names of people by this association technique. Try to make stories as weird as you can.

**APPLICATION:** You may use pegging technique to remember any lists in daily life, office or studies. It is also useful for association of numbers with any list as mentioned above.

## 2) CHUNKING METHOD:

Chunking means breaking long letters, numbers into small pieces so our memory retains it in terms of small chunks. You may find chunking in your daily life in important numbers such as telephone numbers; credit/debit card numbers etc. Just consider following big numbers.

**997860989457 &**

**997-860-989-457**

If you practice, you will realize that second number which is in the form of chunks is easy to memorize.

**APPLICATION**

Chunking method has huge application in daily life, professional life & studies. One application you may see in memorizing spellings and meanings in English. Let's take example of the word **"ASSASSINATION"**. If you ask any people or students to write spelling and ask meaning then more than 70% will fail in writing spelling and telling meaning of the word "ASSASSINATION".

(Image source: From Wikimedia Commons)

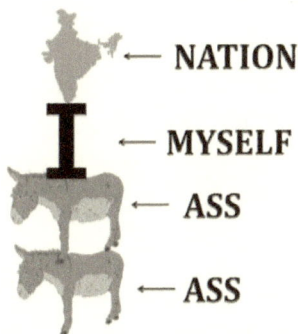

But if you use a simple trick and chunk the word into **ASS-ASS-I-NATION** you may memorize spelling easily. Also if you want to memorize its meaning then you may use **"DISTORTION"** technique as 'There is ASS on ASS on which I am sitting and travelling throughout the NATION and after seeing this I am getting killed by my relatives. This story is distorted hence our brain will catch it and retain it for lifetime. It is also applied in medical terminologies

**Gastroesophageal- Gas-Tro-Eso-Phag-Eal**

## 3) MEMORY ROOT TECHNIQUE

Our brain already has some fixed memories in mind which we can use effectively in memorizing anything. For example you can create your memory root which is fixed in your brain. You may think about journey from home to school, college or office and create fixed sequence of things which you already memorize such as bedroom-kitchen-bathroom-hall-door of hall-steps-parking of society building-gate of society-road-kirana store-auto rickshaw stand-highway-road quadrant-market-bus stop-statue-playground-temple-college etc. Now you can keep associating each place with any object and array of sequence which you want to memorize.

## APPLICATION

If I want to memorize list of Indian Prime ministers in sequence, then I can memorize in a way that Pundit Jawaharlal Nehru who was First Indian Prime Minister who is sleeping in bedroom. Then second Prime Minister Gulzarilal Nanda is having breakfast in kitchen. Next Prime minister Lal Bahadur Shastri is taking bath in bathroom as he was tired then next Prime Minister Indira Gandhi is sitting in hall & reading political news. Next Morarji Desai is ringing bell on door of hall and like this way you can memorize sequence of all prime ministers. You need to consciously have a look on pictures or videos of each prime minister and read brief about them which will put all of them in your long term memory as you are applying senses to memorize them. You may also distort their names if you find some of names difficult to memorize by using distortion techniques.

## 4) KEYWORDS METHOD:

Keywords are important words in passages, definitions or answers and we can memorize entire context on the basis of keywords. Example: If you see following keywords, you can easily make at least a 2 page story if you know the story or have heard about it at least once.

**Boy**

**Wolf**

**Sheep**

**Villagers**

**Morale**

**APPLICATION**

Keywords method is useful to memorize definitions, large paragraphs, languages, vocabulary or long answers which are difficult to memorize by **'Rote'** method. Every passage or long answers have some specific keywords in them which are core part and we can build up other part of passage or answers on the basis of them in a proper sequence. You can use **'Distortion'** technique and make keywords easier to memorize. For example, in history while memorizing facts about Akbar there are following important keywords Akbar-Humayun-Bairam Khan-

Godavari –centralized system-tripled wealth-death Agra. Then we can distort as akhbar (newspaper in Hindi)-hema (actress)-bai(maid)-God(Ganesh) etc.

## 5) LINK METHOD-MEMORY MAP

Firstly we distort the given words and then create a link in them by associating one object with other. We may use story method also in that. It includes encoding the information then associating image with it and then linking or chaining it with other objects.

## APPLICATION

Link method can be used in Science to memorize sources of vitamins, the applications of chemicals etc. Example: If you want to memorize some chemical names as follows:

Carbonate,Sodium,Magnesium,Argon,Fluorine,Bauxite,Ox ygen,Polonium,Cobalt,Chlorine,Gallium then you can first distort them and then can link them. You may also create story. You opened car's bonnet from which soda comes out. You take this soda and cook Maggi in it. Then you put this Maggi in air gun and fire it in sky. After that it falls on floor .You collect it from floor and put it in a box. The box is carried by ox. Then that ox started playing polo game and suddenly Cobra bites him .You apply kala(black) rin(cloth washing soap) on ox when he runs in a galli.You will observe that this story is unique ,humorous and hence your mind will capture it long time.

## 6) RHYTHM METHOD

As per NLP, if we are using our five senses to memorize then memory becomes long term. While most of memory techniques use visual sense, Rhyme Method uses auditory sense to keep information in mind. If we are using rhythms, repetitions, rhymes, song formats melody etc. for memory. This method becomes more effective with distortion and story method.

## APPLICATION

Rhymes can be used absolutely anywhere in your routine such as creating a password, school or college studies, office etc. but only thing required is that you need to be good in vocabulary. We have already used number rhyme above in pegging system. Let's consider few examples. If you want to remember which way to tight a screw then you may make a short poem and give it rhythm such as "Right way its tight way while left way its loose way". If you want to recall the year in which Columbus came in America then you can make a sweet poem as "In 1432;Columbus came in the Ocean Blue".(Here two and blue will make a rhyme, you may give any music to above poem from child videos or songs.)

## 7) STORY METHOD (With Humor)

Our brain easily captures and retains stories, you all will definitely recall stories in your childhood which your granny used to tell or some stories from your school books even if you have learnt them many years ago and even you have not revised them. It's not necessary to be creative for making a story; all of us can make a story to remember anything. Always inculcate distortion and humor in the story.

## APPLICATION

Storytelling is an amazing method while learning science. Especially when at early stage, students are not acquainted with scientific terms, story method along with distortion & humor can create wonders. While memorizing sources of Vitamin A, we may use link method along with distortion. The sources of vitamin A are – liver oil, skim milk, eggs, yellow vegetables & fruits, green vegetables, cheese. Now, we can use link method as follows. First we will always do distortion to make it easy. Let's consider 'A' as any of our friend whose name starts from A –let's take Ankit. Let's distort lever oil as famous Bollywood comedian Johnny Lever, rest of the things don't need distortion as our brain already knows them. Now we will link all of them by creating a story. Ankit meets Johnny Lever sir then gives him a glass of milk. After having milk Johnny lever's big eyes gets converted in eggs & they go on getting bigger & bigger as he keeps on drinking milk. After some time his eyes blasts and from within yellow & red fruits come out. Ankit takes these fruits and goes to the vegetable market of green vegetables where his yellow fruits get easily sold & he purchases cheese from that money. You will always memorize this story as it is weird and your senses are used in this and you will never forget sources of Vitamin A in your life. Next method is Mind mapping which in combination with story method becomes very effective tool.

## 8) MINDMAPPING

On mind maps there are some main entities and some branches to connect from one semi entity to other depending on the sequence of memory or thought process. Each branch is unique in the mind map. With the correct triggers you can always memorize all things. Those trigger points are mentioned in the memory maps. Once you draw mind map, then start paying your attention from one branch to other and reinstate & consolidate the data in your brain. With practice you will be instantly able to recall entire mind map with the help of photographic memory.

## APPLICATION

This is a memory technique or analytical tool which is used in memorizing data, process, flow or drafting our thought process on paper.

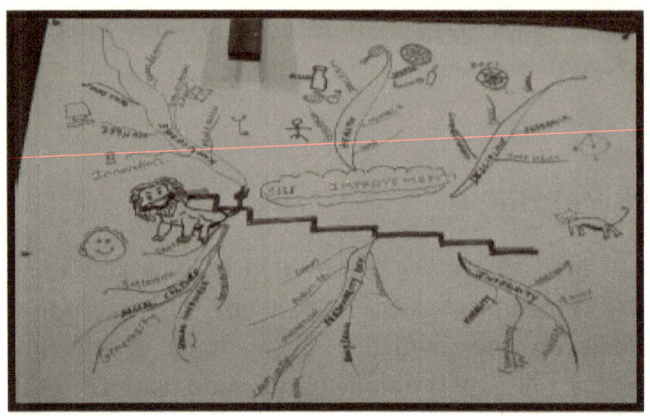

**A Mind map for Self Improvement by participants.**

## 9) BODY MNEMONICS:

Body mnemonics uses **'Kinesthetic'** sense out of our five senses where we use our body, muscles etc. to memorize some theory.

## APPLICATION

In studies of Mathematics and science, body mnemonics are effectively used. For example there was a left hand thumb rule, right hand thumb rule, 3 fingers to indicate mutually perpendicular planes etc.

## 10) LETTER INITIALS OR ACRONYMS AS MNEMONICS:

We can use initials acronyms as mnemonics which makes us memorize things easily. Instead of memorizing entire things, we can memorize initials to memorize data easily.

## APPLICATION

While memorizing difficult terminologies in medical science, chemistry or memorizing specific sequence, we can use acronyms as mnemonics .Example; **'VIBGYOR'** is a famous example used worldwide which is pneumonic to memorize colors of rainbow which are Violet, Indigo, Blue, Green, Yellow, Orange & red. Another famous example can be VBODMAS rule in mathematics for prioritizing mathematical operations. Where V stands for Vinculum, B stands for Bracket; O stands for Of, D stands for Division, M stands for Multiplication, A stands for addition & S stands for subtraction.

## 11) ACROSTICS:

An acrostic is a poem in which original words or terms are distorted and new words are formed according to make a poem with rhythm.

## APPLICATION

Acrostics have multiple applications in studies such as history, geography, science. One example to memorize plants in solar system is ,"My Very Elegant Mom Just Served Us Nine Pastries.", In which planets are - Mercury,Venus,Earth,Mars,Jupiter,Saturn,Uranus,Neptune ,Pluto. Here initials of the words are same.

## 12) DISTORTION :

As you know distortion is by default by our mind and also we can deliberately do it to memorize things. Our mind captures & retains distortion easily.

## APPLICATION

Distortion is a memory technique which can be used for any kind of data to memorize and can be effectively used in combination with other memory techniques. Distortion is used in vocabulary to memorize meaning of English words. Let's consider few examples:

**CAJOL**-Lets distort it as Kajol (Bollywood actress) who is convincing her husband to allow her to work in movies which indicates meaning of the word CAJOL as 'to persuade someone with sweet talks to do something for which they are not ready'.

**JADED**-Distort it as JADA (Fat) and think of any fat person who is tired and exhausted which is the meaning of the word JADED.

**DILIGENT**- I have a friend who is policy 'agent' who stays in 'Delhi'. He is working very hard to get policies for his companies hence indicates the meaning of the word DILIGENT which is hard working.

## APPLICATION OF MULTIPLE MEMORY TECHNIQUES FOR MAPS:

We can use multiple memory techniques to memorize maps. Let's take example of India map. Here our target is to memorize states which are surrounding Maharashtra state. We will be using distortion, story method, and link method for this.

(Image source: Pinterest.com)

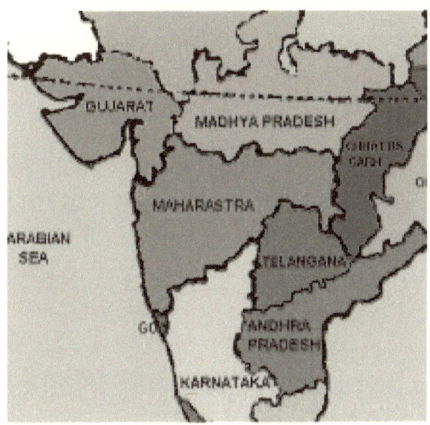

With due respect to all states & our Indian culture, let's Consider sequence as **Maharashtra-Gujrat-MadhyaPradesh-Chattisgar-telangana-Karnataka-Goa.**

Now,lets distort the names Maharashtra as a 'maharaja' who is addicted to alcohol.In 'rat' (night ,distorted from Guj-rat) he goes out of his palace to have madya(distorted from Madhya pradesh means alcohol in hindi or sanskrit).The alcohol is costing 'chattis'(distorted from

Chattisgadh which means 36). In this alcohol he mixes 'tel'(means oil distorted from Telangana).After having this mixture he gets kick and starts doing 'nataka'(means drama in hindi distorted from Karnataka) and finally goes(distorted from Goa).You can see that this story is weird and funny that's why you will always memorise this story.

### 13) NUMBERS TO LETTERS METHOD

Our brain does not catch numbers easily as we are not much associated with numbers. We are human beings & we relate with 3D objects with motion, sound and colors & taste easily. Hence in this 'Numbers to Letters Method' we convert numbers into letters and then letters into objects. It will vary from person to person which letter he or she wants to associate with which number. Consider following association on the basis of visual & auditory senses.

**0-s (as shape of zero is like sun, we are giving it initial of sun)**

**1-t or d (vertical structure)**

**2-n (If you rotate 2 it will look similar to n)**

**3- m (if you rotate 3, it will look similar to m)**

**4-r (as 4 ends with r)**

**5-L (if see border of hands when you make it 5, it will look like L)**

**6- g (if you rotate 6, it will look like g)**

**7-K (If you observe K, there are two 7's joined together)**

**8- v (If you look central part of 8, you will see two v's )**

**9-P (If you take mirror image of 9, it will look like P)**

**10- ts or ds ( t or d for 1 & s for 0)**

## APPLICATION

This is the most effective way to memorize numbers & number related theories. We can memorize absolutely any data related to numbers. In our introductory seminars & memory workshops, we do memorize 100 digit number created by public on the spot within 3 minutes. We can memorize value of π (pi) up to 100 digits after decimals. Important thing is you need to convert all digits from 00 to 100 in objects which are colorful, bold & related with you. We can memorize any phone numbers, credit & debit card numbers, passwords & absolutely any numerical structure with this technique. Let's take example of dates in history.

1853 –The year in which railway service started in India

1-t, 8-v, 5-l, 3-m so we convert 18 53 in tv - lm. We have our objects ready for tv which is television & for lm, we will use lemon. Then, we will create a story from it such as there is a tv & we have put lemon on the tv & as soon as lemon touches tv, the train is coming out from tv which is the first train in India. You may use this technique in pegging also where you need to associate numbers with list.

## THE MEMORY EXERCISES

Exactly as weight training in gym add muscles to our body, similarly following a brain-healthy lifestyle and performing regularly targeted brain exercises can also increase & reserve our brain's cognitive power.

**1. Check Your Memory's Recall Power:** Make a list of anything such as your resolutions, mistakes, and items to purchase from market, name of people etc. The longer the list, better it is. Then after every 2 hours, see how many items you recall. To get better impact, try to make items in list as challenging as possible.

**2. Do Basic Calculations Visually:** Try to do simple addition, multiplication & other mathematical operations without using pen & paper.

**3. Draw a Map:** Whenever you will visit new places, try to draw its map on paper; it will increase your recalling power.

## PERSONAL EXPERIENCE OF AUTHOR:

I used to get surprised that I could remember a poem from my 5th standard whereas I am not able to retain or recall a poem which I wanted to use for one of my presentations even after repetitive attempts! Why it happens that during my school days on 1st August at Lokmanya Tilak Jayanti (Birth Anniversary), I used to forget many points from my speech but at the same time now I can completely narrate story of Geeta Phogat from famous bollywood 'Dangal' movie?

All the answers of this unpredictable nature of memory I could find in memory patterns. As per my upbringing from childhood, my VAK Senses (Visual, Auditory & Kinesthetic) are being moulded to delete & retain specific nature of content. As poems have rhymes & our teacher used to involve kinesthetic movements & gestures into it along with daily repetitions,

I could still memorize poems. About my speech in school time, I was just focusing on conscious 'ROTE' method (rather than connecting my VAK senses) resulting in failures even after repetitions, whereas in Geeta Phogat biopic, while watching movie, I was completely connected with all my VAK senses involved & watching it in flow without any consciousness resulting in memorizing 100% events in the movie. I could write or narrate each & every details from that movie. Also as mentioned in memory cues-visuals & motions appeals to human memory & it can retain & recall things easily without conscious efforts.

I would also like to share my one past drawback of forgetting things frequently. I used to forget mobiles, keys, cash etc. My belief had became that as I am loaded with many things ,such instances are bound to happen, but after mastering in memory techniques, I started associating objects with some imaginary objects with big size. E.g. I started imagining that I am putting keys in a big glass in drawer of table, to memorize drawer as key location. Soon, I got rid of my problem of forgetting things & now I could even recall things of other people in family or in my office. **-Vaibahv Vasant Patil**

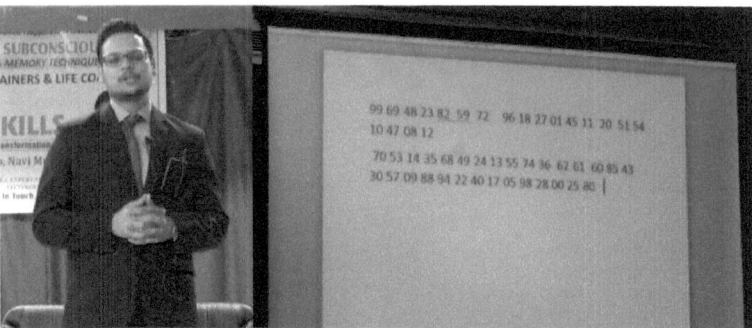

**Memorizing 100 digit number created by public in forward as well as in reverse way within 3 minutes, Navi Mumbai. Always each & every individual present in the audience claps for at least one minute after this 'on the spot demonstration by us'**

*"In the absence of good memory & lack of repetition or revision all learning is in vain"-Vaibhav Vasant Patil*

# PART 4

# ABOUT THE CREATORS OF

# 'THE BLISS'

## ABOUT THE CREATORS OF 'THE BLISS':

The Bliss & its series are published by training company Shareskills Center For Training & Transformation and written by its founders Mr.Vaibhav Vasant Patil & Shruti Chitlangiya Dhruve. It is a known brand for corporate trainings, public workshops and institutes and college level trainings. Under this brand, training modules are created and delivered in various fields by our expert team of trainers. The bliss & its series are also promoted by Shareskillsonline.

## ABOUT SHARESKILLS CENTER FOR TRAINING & TRANSFORMATION

Today's word is all about skills. In personal, professional and academic life skills plays important role. Along with skills, there is also a huge importance of subconscious mind awareness & overall life wellness to keep balance in our life. Many students, higher management people or any common man are not able to cope up with stress & are becoming victims of anxiety, depression, work life imbalance, problems in personal & professional life & relevant health issues such as blood pressure, obesity, cardiac diseases etc. The success of professional as well as personal life depends majorly on our **"Emotional Intelligence" & "Subconscious Mind Management"**.

We at Shareskills Training provide **all types of training programs in corporate, public and institutes by integrating them with NLP & Emotional Intelligence.** We also personally train our elite clients on the **"Subconscious Mind, Emotional Intelligence with relevant NLP (Neuro Linguistic Programming)"**.We serve our diverse, extensive, result oriented, monitorable expert training programs as per personalized needs & problems of the client.

The mission of our organization Shareskills is to work for mass wellness and our vision is that every human being must be aware of, learn and utilize the powers & skills which lies within themselves .Everyone has a right to live the blissful life and no one should suffer from health, mind, relationships or professional issues.

Apart from Public workshops, we give trainings in corporate & college to higher authorities like Founders/Directors, CEOs, Trustees, HOD's, etc. Almost every month we arrange our public workshops in various cities. We give trainings to government officers, students, corporate employees, and college professors under FDP, some patients with specific medical issues or to drug addicts. We also provide webinar based trainings, online content of our training programs, personal counseling & personalized trainings etc.

## About shareskillsonline:

We would also like to mention about our new venture which is an online training company-shareskillsonline - The online version of Shareskills Center For Training & Transformation.

This is an online skills sharing platform where you will get to learn, train or teach and also earn by sharing your skills. On this platform you will get all skills related important aspects of life such as health, career, academics, profession, relationship, wealth and mindfulness. You can connect with our online training programs, live webinars and online courses of shareskillsonline with our website, Facebook page and YouTube. The website of company shareskillsonline and have various courses related to important domains of life by experts in affordable fees. Every course is in lessons and quiz format and E - Certificate is given after successful completion of every course.

We have also created our video content courses on our E-Learning website www.shareskillsonline.com. At this website you will get all courses by experts having specific skills in affordable prices. You will also get E-certificate if complete the courses successfully.

**Moments go memories& impact last forever!**

**It's real feeling of bliss, to open up, empower, heal, counsel & transform people, especially youth**

## BETT MODULES – PUBLIC & CORPORATE TRAINING MODULES BOF SHARESKILLS TRAININGS

| BEHAVIORAL MODULE | EMOTIONAL MODULE | THOUGHT MODULE | TECHNICAL MODULE |
|---|---|---|---|
| • Team Building<br>• Problem solving<br>• Critical thinking<br>• Interpersonal skills<br>• Effective Communication skills<br>• Personality Development<br>• Effective Presentation Skills<br>• Selling skills<br>• Time Management<br>• CRM<br>• Conflict Resolution<br>• Work Life Balance<br>• Self Transformation<br>• Self Improvement<br>• Patience Mastery<br>• Dealing with difficult people<br>• Counseling skills<br>• Email Etiquettes<br>• Interpersonal Skills | • Self-awareness<br>• Emotional Intelligence<br>• Motivation<br>• Stress Management<br>• Positivity From Negativity<br>• Forgiveness to prosperity<br>• Risk management<br>• Effective Communication with Emotions<br>• Empathetic Thinking<br>• Self Love<br>• Emotional Triggers<br>• Emotions To Motivation | • Innovative Thinking<br>• Creative Thinking<br>• Critical Thinking<br>• Strategic Thinking<br>• Selling Skills<br>• Attitude& Mindset<br>• Prioritization<br>• Problem Solving<br>• Ethical Thinking<br>• Positive Thinking<br>• Law Of Attraction<br>• Change Management<br>• Out Of The Box Thinking<br>• Goal Setting | • Computer training<br>• Aptitude<br>• English<br>• Digital Marketing<br>• Facebook Marketing<br>• Govt. Exams Training<br>• Power Point<br>• Microsoft Excel<br>• Microsoft Word<br>• Business Development<br>• CRM<br>• Safety Training<br>• Memory Techniques |

## HOW ARE WE DIFFERENT?

We at Shareskills Trainings provide all types of corporate trainings along with 'NLP & Subconscious Mind' & 'Emotional Intelligence', as subconscious mind & Emotional Intelligence plays almost 80% role in the professional success of Management Or Employees. The NLP Subconscious Mind & Emotional Intelligence Training transforms from within & enhances inner energy, creativity, perspectives, self-image, beliefs, and values of Employees & Management.

**Shareskills Corporate, Public & Institute level Training Module:**

It provides proven tools & techniques to learn how to implement systems that assures long term engagement & retention of employees from our expert trainers across country. Versatile Corporate training modules of 'Shareskills' offers its clients customized, innovative, diverse & abundant options to choose for employees transformation in desired manner, which ultimately leads to paradigm upwards shift in profitability, prosperity & wellbeing of organization. Our public training modules are full of quality & quantity of content and language flexibility. Simplicity is our USP where we deliver public workshops in easiest way with abundant activities. Our institute level training modules majorly consists of soft skills, mindfulness and technical trainings where we conduct trainings in colleges and institutes & also offer courses under college curriculum.

## CORPORATE TRAINING MODULES OF SHARESKILLS

- Short Term Mono-Theme Training with only one topic
- Long Term Package Of Multi-Theme Training with multiple but collateral topics
- Indoor/In-house Training
- Outdoor/Offsite/Outbound Training
- On-job Training
- Online Live/pre-recorded Training
- Pre Training – TNA
- TNA Based Training

- Evaluation Module & Evaluation based training
- Post Training –Follow up Module
- Case Studies based training
- Trainings via shareskillsonline platform

## BENEFITS OF OUR CORPORATE TRAINING MODULE

- Better employee engagement & morale
- Keep up with industry changes
- Be ahead of the competitors
- Remain competitive within the marketplace
- SWOT analysis
- Advance employee skills
- Increased satisfaction & motivation level
- Attract new talent & retain best talent
- Provide internal promotion opportunities & relevant cost saving
- Increased efficiencies in manpower
- Increased capacity to learn & practice new things
- Increased innovation in strategies and products
- Reduced employee turnover/attrition
- Enhanced company image & relevant brand equity
- Advanced level soft skills & communication skills

## PUBLIC WORKSHOP MODULES OF SHARESSKILLS THROUGHOUT THE YEAR

- Introductory workshops per month
- 2 day basic wellness Course
- 2 days basic NLP Practitioner for self-course
- 2 days basic Emotional Intelligence course

- 1 day courses on any topic in BETT Module
- 5 Days advance level course in special domain
- Outbound training programs for public & corporate
- Webinar based counseling & training
- Personalized training
- Training with our pre-recorded videos
- Trainings via shareskillsonline platform

**BENEFITS OF OUR PUBLIC TRAINING MODULE**

- Holistic wellness in life in all important domains
- Self-healing with power of mind
- Improved confidence & self-image
- Get rid of allergy, phobia, bad habits on the spot
- Memory training for all students & professionals
- Improved relations in personal & professional life
- Changed belief system
- Erasing past painful memories & living in presence
- Emotional intelligence for personal & professional life
- Protecting self from others emotionally
- Never ending motivation in life
- Soft skills & communication skills
- NLP,EI & Along with memory techniques
- Effective Parenting or couple counseling
- Trainings via shareskillsonline platform

## INSTITUTE/COLLEGE MODULES OF SHARESSKILLS THROUGHOUT THE YEAR (FOR STUDENTS, TEACHERS AS WELL AS NON TEACHING STAFF)

- Free Introductory workshops in colleges
- 2 day basic wellness course
- 2 days basic NLP Practitioner for self-course
- 2 days basic Emotional Intelligence course
- 1 day courses on any topic in BETT Module
- 5 Days advance level course in special domain
- Outbound training programs & industrial visits
- Webinar based counseling & training
- Personalized training
- Training with our prerecorded videos
- Trainings via shareskillsonline platform

## BENEFITS OF OUR INSTITUTE/COLLEGE TRAINING MODULE (FOR STUDENTS, TEACHERS AS WELL AS NON -TEACHING STAFF)

- Holistic wellness in life of students or faculties
- Self-healing with power of mind
- Improved confidence &self-image
- Get rid of allergy, phobia, bad habits on the spot
- Memory training for all students & professionals
- Improved relations in personal & professional life
- Changed belief system & improved confidence
- Erasing past painful memories & living in presence with evergreen smile.

- Emotional intelligence for personal & professional life to deal with frustrations and failures
- Protecting self from others emotionally
- Never ending motivation in life
- Soft skills & communication skills
- NLP,EI & Along with memory techniques
- Better self-discipline in students and staff
- Better performance of teachers with our Teachers Training Module
- Better motivation for students to do extracurricular and co-curricular activities.

**Happy & satisfied participants are our ultimate goal.**

**(A moment from Navi Mumbai)**

Highlights of our 2 days workshop which is high on demand.

Snapshot of our personalized training program.

NLP,Emotional Intelligence & Memory Techniques by Shruti Dhruve Chitlangia & Vaibahv Patil

875 views

Shruti Vaibhav
Published on Mar 28, 2019

Our YouTube channel 'shareskillsonline –All skills at one platform" is the best medium to connect with clients with free content & updates about our upcoming programs.

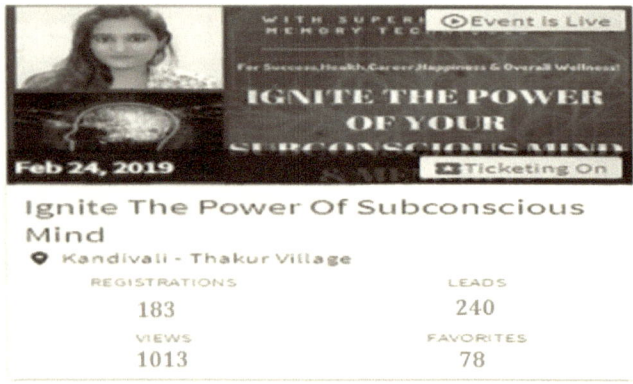

We are presently connect with public on all available platforms such as Events high, Mera events, FB Ads etc.

# FACEBOOK ADS MASTERY

Learn To Use 'Cost Effective' FB ADS To Reach Your Customers & Grow Your Business.

## AT THANE NOW

## 1 DAY PRACTICAL WORKSHOP

### FOR ALL TRAINERS & ENTREPRENEURS

THE PARTICIPANTS WILL BE ABLE TO :

- To Create Landing Page Ads & Get Leads On Social Media
- To Create Leads Ads & Get Leads In Excel Sheet Format
- To Understand FB Ads System, To Design Compatible Ads/Images As Per FB Policy & To Use For Your FB Page
- To Create & Boost Posts, Crucial Events Effectively
- To Analyse Clients Responses For Ads & To Autoreply

*ALSO YOU CAN OUTSOURCE US YOUR FB PAGE AT CHEAPEST RATE EVER!

Our exclusive Facebook Mastery workshop is hit among trainers & entrepreneurs.

## TESTIMONIALS FROM SOME OF OUR CLIENTS:

### 1. VARSHA BANGAR

**(Maharashtra Govt. Class A Officer – Asst. Director, Maharashtra Finance & Accounts Service)**

I completed engineering and MBA from top institutes in Mumbai and got a good, high paying, lucrative job. Since my father is in Government service, it was always my dream to become a top level Government Officer. Hence, I left my job and started preparing for civil services examinations. Before marriage, I worked very hard; I even qualified in preliminary stages but could not qualify in mains examination. My marriage happened, I got a baby. My brother and sister, who started preparing for civil services examinations after me & under my guidance, both got selected. I was not jealous of them but yet very much frustrated with myself. My confidence, self-image, beliefs started devaluating. Preparing for competitive exams while balancing home & family after marriage was challenging. Every year since I commenced preparing for exams, I used to get selected in preliminary examination but success eluded me in later stage of exams. I had almost lost hopes and belief in myself. But I am fortunate that I attended introductory workshops of Shareskills in Mumbai and there I got an intuition that here lies solution to my problem!

I enrolled for 2 days and 5 days workshops and got a 360 degree core transformation in my belief system and I changed language with myself. I am thankful to Vaibhav sir & Shruti madam who gave me personalized training for preparing my mind to crack different levels of exam stages.

I learned to reprogram my mind in tune with my goal. Today I am a Government Officer and also preparing for higher level exams and 100% confident that I am going to excel in my field & contribute my best to my state & country. Now, I practice all life wellness techniques given by Shareskills on me & also on my family members for their wellness.

## 2. GURUJAN SINGH

### (National level Volleyball player)

Volleyball is life for me. I used to play lot of volleyball matches. But I used to get demotivated and depressed after a loss. I was even facing consistent physical fitness problems.

That time when I attended introductory workshops of Shruti madam, I realized that win and loss is part and parcel of game &the same applies to our lives as well. I also understood how my body pain was related with my mind. You need to find positive intention in whatever happens with you. An important thing is enjoying what you do.

I completely changed and began to live in the present instead of dwelling in past & worrying about future.NLP & Emotional intelligence also had positive impact on my health and work life balance. Now I am living a satisfactory life as railway employee and I also guide youngsters for volleyball championships.

## 3. SANDIP PATIL

### (Senior Police Officer)

Being in police department, in my initial days it was getting tougher for me to get adjusted to my job and other stress factors going with it. I was unable to do my job with satisfaction and conviction and something was holding me back. My work life balance was pathetic. But when I attended introductory workshop and learnt about stress management and emotional intelligence from Shruti madam and Vaibhav sir, I felt as if I have got a magical genie which was my own mind who can solve my problems. My work life balance improved a lot. My professional as well as personal relationship started improving which increased my efficiency & output in my job. I am thankful to Shruti madam & Vaibhav sir for giving me a lifetime gift of NLP & Emotional Intelligence.

## 4. SONU KESHARI

### (Entrepreneur, Music company owner)

Becoming an entrepreneur has always been my dream but I had some limiting beliefs due to my past experiences and from anti-rich mindset of people with whom I grew up. I always wanted to do something extraordinary in my career, but my perceptions were holding me back. In personalized training sessions when Shruti madam explained why and how we should change our limiting beliefs, it was an eye opener for me. **Glass walk & Fire walk** activity conducted in a belief change workshop was amazing and convincingly could sow the seeds of new empowering beliefs in me. Also techniques & activities for abundance and financial freedom worked as additional boosters for my business & my revenues. Some NLP techniques have helped me a lot in inculcating creativity in my music business where I could think like my idols. It was a magic, where I could model the business model, thinking patterns and styles of my idols.

## 5. DR.MAHESH GOUR SIR

**(CA & Financial Consultant, Senior ICAI Member & faculty, Founder –Gaur's E-Learning)**

I know Shruti madam from the time when she used to be my student. She is extremely brilliant, outspoken, excellent presenter and always in merit. Even though I was her teacher, I must say I have learnt a lot of things from her.

When she talked with me about NLP & Emotional Intelligence in our routine discussions, the concept of subconscious mind just hit my mind hard. I started following the tips and techniques recommended by her for my new endearing business. I think although I was excellent as far as technical knowledge and creativity as CA, still somewhere I needed to align my thoughts, neurons & behaviors in tune with our goals and visions by ensuring I have ignited my subconscious mind towards it. Now I always explore new & innovative ideas in my new E- learning educational institute. I am thankful to Shareskills and Shruti madam for introducing a new effective tool of NLP in my skill set. Also Emotional Intelligence tips given by her even in casual talks were also helpful for me. As I work 24 x 7 for my routine lectures and my new E-Learning business, emotionally & physically it used to drain me, but when I started using Emotional Intelligence tools in my work and personal life, my life became sorted like never before. Now, I am just touching new heights in my freelancing job, book publishing, CA consultancy & E-Learning business as well.

## 6. SARIKA KANSE-PAWAR

### (Railway Police, Mumbai)

Being a married woman it was getting tough for me especially after pregnancy to manage my family and highly time centric shift based hectic job such as railway police. I was about to give up my job and focus on my husband and two babies. In our family, people started blaming me that I don't care for my baby. But then luckily I met Vaibhav sir in one of his seminars in which he spoke about work-life balance and how one should live in 'being self ' rather than ' living in role' of wife or mother. Also Shruti madam's own life experiences motivated me and I decided and made up my mind to face the challenges in front of me and not to give up my job which is my dignified identity and also a stable, secure income source which would have been definitely important .They both are very empathetic and always counseled me in my tough times.

## 7. DR.NIVEDITA PATIL.

**(Senior eye surgeon, life coach, corporate trainer)**

Being a doctor by profession that too an eye surgeon, requires to establish good rapport with patients so as to make them mentally ready for sensitive eyes operation and also for customer retention and good word of mouth. With experience I have already learnt about rapport building but rapport building with NLP & EI in Shareskills Training programs was more impactful. I could diminish or even vanish the fear, stress and anxiety of operation from patients mind few days before surgery with better communication.

On a personal note, when I started connecting with my subconscious mind for my work, it enhanced my health, fitness, efficiency, capacity, patience, controlled emotions which resulted nicely in my post operations results.NLP & EI is sea of useful information & with good trainers like Shruti & Vaibhav, and these tools have power to transform lives of people. Apart from medical specialist, I am also a life coach & corporate trainer. I have attended various training programs but I would like to mention one unique thing about Shareskills is that the male-female trainer combination is just perfect & I enjoy each and every minutes of training programs of Shareskills

## 8. DR.NILESH MESHRAM.

### (Senior orthopedic surgeon)

There is a deep connect between the human mind and body. I have seen patients who feel pain even due to the thought of injury or accidents. NLP has helped me a lot for their holistic healing i.e. physical and mental healing.NLP, subconscious imprints and emotional intelligence has multiple utility in medical profession, especially orthopedics where actually we don't heal patients with medicines and surgeries but its belief of patients in our medicines and surgeries which actually heal them.

Even after I have attended all training programs of Shareskills, I still don't lose any opportunity to attend them repetitively because every time I learnt something new which I can apply and enhance my skills. In terms of NLP tools for health & wellness, I have found a complementary thing which is becoming a boon for my patients.

## 9. ANAND MORE

### (Body builder & gym trainer, Mumbai)

Body building is a profession where we require a lot of mental & physical toughness. We also go through a lot of emotional ups and downs where we need to compromise a lot in life. We need to compromise on our time, our eating likes & dislikes etc. We also need to maintain relationship with other people while remaining in this profession for example, our parents & relatives might oppose us or start talking negative about us & our profession. Shruti madam taught me how to mute external & inner critical voices. We need to inculcate discipline in our life in diet, sleep etc. which requires a lot of control on our mind. NLP training by Shruti madam & Vaibhav sir is very powerful and impactful which changed my belief system & transformation in life towards overall wellbeing. Now, I have won many body building tournaments & all credit I devote to Vaibhav sir, Shruti madam & Shareskills team.

## 10. NIMESH CHHEDA

### (3 Degree Astrologer Consultant)

Astrology is not only about knowledge but it is also about counseling and healing people on the basis of it. Although I was good as far as knowledge is concerned but somewhere I felt that I need to be more emotionally intelligent to get awareness of my own emotions as well as emotions of my clients so that I can manage them well. Fortunately I got opportunity to get personalized counseling by Shruti madam and within just one sitting I could see major transformation in my thinking and confidence. I just followed all techniques daily and I can say that I reinvented myself. Now, apart from my regular middle class and lower middle class clients, I also have elite clients which are only possible due to reprogramming my mind and relevant techniques. If you want to take giant leap in your life then I will definitely suggest attending at least introductory workshop and experiencing intuitions of your mind to learn more from Shruti madam and Vaibhav sir.

## ABOUT TRAINING COMBO OF VAIBHAV SIR & SHRUTI MADAM:

Mr.Vaibhav Vasant Patil & Shruti Chitlangiya Dhruve is a leading pair of trainers in public as well as corporate domains. They both are basically freelancing professors in institutes & in colleges. They both have more than 10 years of experience in their teaching profession. Vaibhav sir has his own organization for competitive exams having tie-ups with many of college centers & private coaching centers in Mumbai, Navi Mumbai, Pune & Karad. Shruti madam is senior faculty in prestigious institutes of CA, ACCA, CS, Competitive exams etc & her goodwill is widely spread in almost every big city of India.

To pursue their dream to make difference in lives of people, they took professional trainings from various national and international institutes regarding life wellness. Together they have transformed life of more than 75,000 students and participants from their teaching & training domains, given more than 200 seminars, have conducted more than 100 workshops and healed many clients with personalized counseling and training. Their skills are complementary to each other and hence together they form a super combination which creates best & long lasting impact in their training programs.

They both promote & run Shareskills Center for training & transformation as Founders & top management along with their core team. They also work together for their online venture shareskillsonline.com which is a hub for many life changing courses on special skills by experts.

**ABOUT VAIBHAV VASANT PATIL**

**Mr.Vaibhav Vasant Patil (BE, MBA)**

**Certified NLP Practitioner, Emotional Intelligence Expert, Author, Business Coach, Digital marketing expert, Memory Guru, Founder-Shareskills Trainings**

He has always been multitalented & versatile student throughout his career. He is basically an Engineering Graduate (B.E. Mechanical) followed by MBA in marketing. He is excellent & a proven leader since his student phase & well versed with extracurricular activities such as Paper presentations, Management events etc. He has rich industrial & managerial experience in Mahindra & Mahindra Automotive. He owns an Educational organization **'Asha Competitive Careers'** spanning all over Maharashtra as tie up with colleges & private institutes. He has huge expertise as technocrat & very successful as an educationalist & as an entrepreneur. He is experienced (around 10+ years) in competitive exams domains with areas of interest in subjects of Quantitative Aptitude, Logic, Arithmetic, Data Interpretation, Career Counseling, GD/PI guidance

&training in Exams like UPSC, MPSC, MBA CET, Railway, Banking, IBPS. He is highly balanced in hard working & smart working. In 2014 he published his multicolor book UPSC-MPSC CSAT which is very useful for competitive exams students.

Now, transforming life of people towards best, through academic guidance & overall Training, is his purpose of life. With rich industry, corporate experience & teaching training experience as senior faculty in prestigious national institutes & in colleges, Vaibhav has thorough insights in entrepreneurship, business coaching, professional skills, motivation, employee morale training needs & this spontaneously & effortlessly pushes him to dynamically structure, innovate, design & redesign all his training programs which have its own benchmarks, sophistication, style & standards.

He is versatile, multitalented & multitasking trainer; hence apart from his core specialization domain in corporate skills, Leadership, Strategizing, Teamwork, Selling skills, Marketing & Branding, he also has his hearty liking & interest for other complementary areas such as Work-Life Balance, Life Skills, Positive Thinking, Time Management, Prioritizing priorities, Relationship Management & many others along with NLP.

Vaibhav has prime focus on long term, continuous self-improvement of his clients, participants or relevant organizations which ensures a timely follow-up, feedbacks & keeping in loop mechanism developed by him. From perspectives of his clients, he has high quality & impactful content, energizing skills, great visualizer, a great source of motivation due to his rich industry, corporate & entrepreneurial experience & career avenues he has chosen which have made his programs & seminars very interactive, engaging, energetic, correlating, empathizing, time flow forgetting & a consistent record of Hit! In addition to his bottom of the heart passion towards training profession, for better authenticity & expertise, he has pursued his **Advanced Diploma In "Train The Trainer"** Certified comprehensive Course from Mumbai. His trademark is "Self- belief & hard work will always lead to prosperity in life". To develop his specific area of expertise in NLP & EI to make his skill more relevant & applicable to his audience, he has completed two exclusive & in depth NLP & Subconscious mind Certified Trainings professional diploma courses from Mumbai. He has also pursued Diploma In "Emotional Intelligence Mastery" From Mumbai. He is a successful digital marketer in addition to his marketing skills as marketing professional. He is founder of Shareskills Center for Training & Transformation which is a leading training company now.

Vaibhav sir taking workshop 'Removing examination phobia with NLP, EI & mind power', K.J. Somaiya College, Mumbai

Record breaking youth attends unique workshop on 'cracking competitive exams with subconscious mind & memory techniques' by Vaibhav Sir.

Vaibhav Sir (Left end), in publication ceremony of his first book 'UPSC-MPSC CSAT' in 2014 in hands of renowned social worker Sindhutai Sapkal in Pune

The publishing ceremony of "The Bliss" Paperback Version

## ABOUT SHRUTI CHITLANGIYA DHRUVE:

**Shute Chitlangiya Dhruve**

**(CS, MBA, M.Com)**

**Certified NLP Practitioner, Emotional Intelligence Expert, Author, Life Coach, Memory Guru, Founder-Shareskills Trainings**

Shruti is a self-transformation cum Wellness coach, specialized in NLP & Subconscious Mind Training & Instinctive Personality Development Trainer. She is highly dedicated public as well as corporate trainer who believes "Life is only a reflection of what we allow and endeavor ourselves to see". Her mature & rational interpersonal skills, pleasant personality attributes, encourages and motivates any ordinary individual to become best version of himself/herself in all possible aspects and ensures strong urge for self-transformation and relevant course of action by him/her towards overall wellbeing.

The core principle and value of Shruti is that a training session should be beneficial, result oriented, relevant to the respective TNA and they should be practical enough for participants to execute it straightway; if training is too theoretical, it rarely makes impact unless it is executed in the form of real life examples and activities to inspire people.

Shruti is virtuous, versatile person gifted with excellent communication skills, smart and pleasant personality which creates huge impact and ensures 100% engagement of her participants. She is a trainer of highest integrity and conviction which ensures purely interactive and lively training sessions with proven highest level of interest among participants. She is strong believer of rationality, practicality and scientific approach towards each aspect of life hence her messages, takeaways, appeals, key points in training sessions and workshops are authentic, reliable, result oriented value for money and with excellent ROI for any client.

She is very knowledgeable and presentable, highly experienced (around 12 years) professional subject trainer with areas of interest in subjects of CA,ACCA, CS, Competitive Careers Exams like MBA Cet, Banking, CPT, IBPS, Commerce and Law related subjects. She is highly balanced in hard working and smart working. She is very effective and efficient proven leader who always promote team work and assigning right work to a right team member which results in accomplishing the given task in right and optimized way and now, transforming life of people through Trainings, is her purpose of life.

With rich academic teaching and training experience as senior faculty in prestigious National and International Institutes, Shruti has thorough insights on various skills needs which spontaneously and effortlessly pushes her to dynamically structure and design all her training programs which has its own benchmarks, sophistication, style and standards. She is versatile, multitalented and multitasking trainer, hence apart from her core specialization domains; her work also includes areas such as Work-Life balance, Life skills, Positive Thinking, Time Management, Prioritizing Priorities, Relationship Management & many others. Shruti has prime focus in long term, continuous self-improvement of her clients and participants which ensures a timely follow up, feedbacks and keeping in loop mechanism developed by her. From perspectives of her clients, she is highly engaging storyteller, great visualizer, a pleasant healer via her words, a great source of motivation due to her personality traits & life fluctuations, a life disciplinarian which have made her programs and seminars very interactive, engaging, energetic, correlating, empathizing, time flow forgetting and a consistent record of Hit!

In addition to her passion towards training profession, for better authenticity and expertise, she has pursued her Advanced Diploma in "Train The Trainer" Certified

Comprehensive Course from Mumbai. Her trademark is "great personality leads to greater prosperity in all aspects of life".

To hone her skills and to make it more relevant and applicable to her audience, she has completed NLP Master Practitioner Program from Mumbai. She has also pursued her Diploma in "Emotional Intelligence Mastery" from Mumbai to perfect her skills and to make her training sessions more participants oriented.

In addition to her freelancing lectureship in prestigious institutes, she is a co-founder of Shareskills.

You can follow Shruti madam on the following social media platforms:

YouTube/shrutichitlangiyadhruve

Face book/shrutichitlangiyadhruve

Telegram/shrutichitlangiyadhruve

instagram/shruti.cd

www.shrutichitlangiyadhruve.com

shrutichitlangiyadhruve@gmail.com

Shruti madam has got immense talent in conducting icebreaking sessions,physical activities, energizers etc.-Suhas Sargar (Motivational Speaker,Mumbai)

Shruti madam getting award as best faculty for ACCA

## GET IN TOUCH WITH US!

**You can get in touch with us through:**

- **Email Id :** shareskillstrainings@gmail.com  or
  info@shareskillsonline.com
- **Website :**
  www.shareskillsonline.com,
  www.shareskillsonline.com

- **Face book page :**
  Shareskills Center For Training & Transformation

- **YouTube :**
  Please like & Subscribe our channel
  **'Shareskillsonline –All skills at one platform'**

- **Instagram : shareskills.trainings**

- **Telegram :** Shareskills.Trainings
- **LinkedIn:**
  https://www.linkedin.com/company/shareskills-center-for-training-transformation

- **The Bliss :** Amazon Kindle, E-book , Audiobook
  Paperback & Hardcover versions available at
  shareskillsonline.com, Amazon.in, flipkart.com
- **Contact No :** 9967509792
- **Our Offices :** Kharghar, Borivali, Karad

www.ingramcontent.com/pod-product-compliance
Lightning Source LLC
Chambersburg PA
CBHW020315290526
45785CB00007B/2806

* 9 7 8 1 0 7 9 2 1 8 1 1 4 *